# The Subaltern Officer of the Prince of Wales's Volunteers

DAY BEGAN TO DAWN

# The Subaltern Officer of the Prince of Wales's Volunteers

The Reminiscences of an Officer of
HM 82nd Foot During the Peninsular War

Including A Brief History of the
82nd Regiment in the Age of Napoleon
by Brevet-Major Jarvis

George Wood

*The Subaltern Officer of the Prince of Wales's Volunteers: the Reminiscences of an Officer of HM 82nd Foot During the Peninsular War*
by George Wood

Including
*A Brief History of the 82nd Regiment in the Age of Napoleon*
by Brevet-Major Jarvis

Originally published in 1825 under the title
*The Subaltern Officer*

*A Brief History of the 82nd Regiment in the Age of Napoleon*
is an adaptation by the Leonaur editors of part of
*Historical Record of the Eighty-Second Regiment or Prince of Wales's Voluntreers*
by Brevet Major Jarvis
published in 1866

Leonaur is an imprint of Oakpast Ltd



ISBN: 978-1-84677-904-6 (hardcover)
ISBN: 978-1-84677-903-9 (softcover)

**http://www.leonaur.com**

**Publisher's Notes**

# Contents

# Preface

If my condescending readers, in taking up this Narrative, entertain an expectation of finding any thing to delight them in style and composition—any of the graces of diction, or flowers of language—they will be greatly disappointed. I am aware of my inability to gratify them in this respect; and sensible that any pretensions whatever of a literary nature, on my part, would be completely ridiculous, because I am sure they would be wholly unfounded:

*————Rude am I in speech,*
*And little bless'd with the set phrase of peace;*
*For, since these arms had first their manly growth,*
*Till now, some few years wasted, they have used*
*Their dearest action in the tented field;*
*And little of this great world can I speak,*
*Save what pertains to feats of broil and battle.*

Let me hope, therefore, that this confession of my incapacity will have its due weight with the critic (if, indeed, any critic can be found who will stoop to notice such a production as mine); that he will be merciful in proportion as he is mighty, and will not seek "to break a butterfly upon the wheel." He cannot, I assure him, think more humbly of my little work, than I do myself.

To the reader who is unacquainted with military affairs I would observe, that in *The Subaltern Officer*, he will find a plain unvarnished account of the different adventures and scenes described in the course of the narrative, which, whatever be its other demerits, can at least lay claim to truth and accuracy: nor will it, I trust, be found without its share of novelty. The journals and memoirs of private soldiers have been frequently published; but not those of subaltern officers, on whom so much depends, and whose duties are of a different nature, and far more arduous than those imposed upon individuals in the ranks. Indeed, one principal object which I have had in view, has been to correct the too general misapprehension, that the sufferings and hardships of war are almost exclusively the lot of the private soldier. Those who peruse the following pages will perceive, that persons in the situation which I had the honour to fill in the army during the most eventful period of my country's struggles, were no less exposed to pains and privations than those placed under them; besides having to contend with the mental anxiety arising from a much greater degree of responsibility.

I have endeavoured, in the present narrative, to avoid technicalities as much as possible, as they might appear obscure to the general reader. It will also be observed, that I have not paid any attention to dates in recounting the adventures detailed; being unwilling, as I had not kept memorandums to ensure correctness on this head, to trust to conjecture, in what, if mentioned at all, ought to be mentioned with precision. There is, moreover, a degree of fashion in omitting such data: but I have avoided the introduction of them not merely for these reasons. As my readers, however, may not be fond of ambiguities, I hope, by a candid confession of one principal motive that has influenced me in this omission, to obtain from them an excuse for what I trust will be considered a pardonable weakness. A widower, not yet "sunk into the vale of years,"—not insensible to the bewitching smile of Beauty, nor altogether hopeless of finding favour in her eyes—I, like many others, try to steal a few years from Father Time, which I should not be so well able to do, did I confine myself strictly to dates.

This narrative was written some few years since; and would have been submitted to the public much earlier, had circumstances allowed: I, however, hope it is not even now too late to do that which may in the least degree afford them amusement; and if the events here related are not so fresh in the memory as they were at the period of their occurring, their narration will at least have the effect of reviving, in the minds of Britons, those deeds of arms which by them never should, and I trust never will, be forgotten. For although a nation be wrapped in profound tranquillity, such a nation as this, which has been justly styled "The anchor and hope of the world!" should not permit a single spark of its martial spirit to expire. Indeed, in a time of peace, it should be even more on the alert, to stimulate the rising generation to heroic feeling, by keeping that national fire alive which has blazed so conspicuously in the hour of need, and which, I trust, no time will damp and no foe extinguish.

These, then, are the principal reasons which have induced me to lay my humble production before the public, with a view of having the honour to add my mite to the many who have contributed to the renown and glory of England. May her laurels, her character, her liberties, and her blessings, ever remain undiminished!

## Chapter 1

# An Ensign Steps Out

*The morning's sun is gleaming bright,*
*And Britain's flag is waving tight,*
*And widely where the gales invite*
*The charger's mane is flowing.*
*Around is many a staring face*
*Of envious boor and wondering grace,*
*And Echo shouts through all the place,*
*"The soldiers be a-going."*

Etonian

On sitting down quietly by our own fire-side, after the fatigues of an active life, our reflections generally turn towards the chequered and various events of the past; and, should these deviate from the common track, they may, by being recorded, prove entertaining and instructive to those who have not moved in the same sphere, and recall to the minds of those who have, gratifying recollections of their profession. In hopes, therefore, that my present undertaking may in some measure answer these purposes, I proceed with my narrative.

In the first place, I shall merely mention that I am the son of an officer in the Army, of an ancient Irish family, but an Englishman by birth. I commenced my military career with an Ensigncy in the Line, and immediately joined my regiment at Uxbridge. I was, I must confess, much struck with the new mode of life I was about to lead, from its apparent splendour. Impressed as I was with the high opinion I had formed of the military profession, I conceived no other could equal it in point of pleasure, idleness, and grandeur: all around me seemed gaiety, freedom, and ease; in fact, it was that kind of life, of all others, best agreeing with my disposition, and I fancied myself one of the most enviable young men in existence; but, like every thing in this mutable world, my dream of happiness was of short duration, as will be seen in the course of events.

I imagined I had only to order, and be obeyed; and, to support these consequential ideas, I assumed an appearance I could not afford, living at the same rate as those gentlemen who possessed independent fortunes, and spending fifteen shillings a-day, when, in reality, I had not more than five; so deceived was I by false appearances and want of experience. It is to be hoped this, and other confessions of my errors, will not be lost on those young officers who are liable to commit similar follies; it is my wish to warn them against those irregularities, which they will presently see experience alone taught me to avoid. But, before I proceed, let me consider what confessions I am about to make: why, those of my past follies, for the caution of others; by which means I necessarily expose my own. Be it so: as I am not ashamed of any transaction, I shall not be deterred by the animadversion, even of the most censorious; let him examine his own passage through the busy scenes of life, and say, whether he has not also been subject to the inadvertencies and frailties of human nature.

Not to digress farther; I was now at the head-quarters of my corps, and in a few days was ordered to mount the uniform of my regiment. This welcome command was joyfully and quickly obeyed, from the delightful anticipation of the fine figure I flattered myself I should make in my gay attire. I desired my servant to take my coat immediately, and have the epaulette sewed on; but, whether he did it himself, whether the tailor had been making too free with the bottle, or whether it was done for the joke's sake, I know not, but it had been sewn on the wrong shoulder; the belt was consequently put on wrong, and the sword hung on the wrong side. Never having worn a red coat before, not even in the Volunteers, I was a perfect novice in the military art; therefore, to the parade I strutted, with my left shoulder decorated more like that of an *Aid-de-camp* than a Subaltern Officer. After having been the laughing-stock of the parade for some time, a friend came and told me of my ridiculous appearance. Conceive my chagrin when I found out the cause of their mirth! I ran off the ground as fast as I could, and had my dress altered as if by magic, for in less than ten minutes I was again on the parade; but my astonishment and shame were heightened on finding myself in a more ludicrous predicament than before; for my servant, in his great hurry, had left all the threads sticking in the shoulder that the epaulette had been removed from, and, in my confusion, I did not observe this fresh disgrace, but made my re-appearance accordingly. By this time the Colonel had arrived; of course his attention was directed towards me, as a newcomer, and he very soon accosted me with a satirical smile, "So, Sir, you have made your first appearance with a turned coat?"

"A turned coat, Sir?" replied I; "I do not know what you mean: I hope, Sir, I shall never be found a turn-coat."

"Why," said he, "you have epaulette holes and threads on your left shoulder, which plainly shows your coat has been turned."

Just as I was going to explain, the drum beat to fall in, so that I had not an opportunity of convincing him to the contrary; but my pride was so much hurt, that I took care to clear up the mistake to my friends, which, I suppose, reached my commanding officer, as he never mentioned the circumstance afterwards.

Here, then, commenced my life as a soldier, from the time of getting my commission until that of my becoming a reduced Captain, which it has been my good fortune to attain from actual service, in about seven years, without money or interest, being, in every sense of the word, a soldier of Fortune, though that lady has now left me in the back-ground, having no farther occasion for my services in the pursuits of war.

I remained in these, my first quarters, in rather an unpleasant state; for being, as I before observed, quite a novice in my new profession, it was necessary to give me some instruction, for which purpose I was sent to drill every morning at six o'clock;

at which exercise I remained about three hours, and to my comfort was placed in the awkward squad, with strict orders to rise gradually, till I was reported by the Adjutant fit for duty. This little difficulty was got over in about six weeks; nor did it at all curb my pleasures, for I used to drink at the mess as long as I could sit, and enjoy every amusement. It happened one night, as I was going to my quarters, about two miles distant, very much the worse for tippling, I fell asleep on the battlements of a bridge. A person who was passing at the time, seeing me in danger, pulled me off, when, being very pot-valiant, I immediately drew my sword, thinking it was some one going to rob me. The man ran away, and while engaged in pursuit of him, I fell down on the road, and there went to sleep; but the mail-coach coming by soon after, the coachman pulled up, and cut me with his whip to wake me, in which he succeeded. I proceeded some distance on my way, when sleep again overpowered me; and on waking in the morning, I found myself in a wet ditch, and a very pretty figure I cut till I changed my dress for parade. This was my kind of life while in my first quarters; when all of a sudden the route came, and we were ordered to march the next morning at five o'clock. It is almost impossible for one who has not witnessed the scene to form an adequate idea of the convulsion of a regiment at this critical juncture. Every person and every thing appears, at such a time, in the utmost confusion; but the principal cause of alarm is the presence of so many creditors for the payment of their bills, and the scarcity of money to meet their demands. Next to this, are the severe pangs felt at parting with sweethearts, and in this agreeable place these were experienced in an extraordinary degree; for the corps having been stationed at Uxbridge a great length of time, there was scarcely one, from the splendid epaulette to the quivering fife, that had not charmed the heart of some sweet maid of this dear town. The morning soon began to dawn,—the baggage already towered on the creaking wagons: the women and children scaled the massive pile,—where seated, they might enjoy their short pipe and little bottle, as they slowly moved along the weary way. The lively bugle sounding the well-known general, plainly told the sorrowful tale that "the soldiers were a-going." Then came the trying scene: the lovely lasses taking their last farewell, and clinging to their dejected lovers—crying, fainting, sighing, till another sound summoned them to tear themselves away. Poor girls! they shrieked, implored, entreated. Another sound! the soldiers are gone; but the dear creatures are resolved to follow. Such, however, was the concourse of despairing maidens, that precaution was found necessary, and sentries were placed at each end of the bridge to prevent their passing: but even this had not the desired effect; they rushed by the guard—but being unable to pass the next, one of these damsels, in despair, scaled the battlements and plunged into the water, making an effort to swim after her desponding lover: but the struggle was vain; she was with difficulty taken out almost a corpse, and restored to her hapless parents. These trying scenes I afterwards found of frequent occurrence in military life; but certainly their first appearance was not calculated to give me any very unfavourable impression of it.

We set off on our march for Derby, where we were stationed some time. Here I still practised the same extravagance as before,—spending "half a crown out of sixpence a-day;" but this excess could not last long. I had only been in this town about a month, when, an order arrived for a Captain, two Subalterns, and one hundred men, to join the first Battalion, which was then at Cork, forthwith.

I must here notice a circumstance which had nearly blasted my future prospects in the Army. Some malicious person, by way, I suppose, of ingratiating himself with the Commanding Officer, informed him I had designated him an old fool; and, to my great astonishment, being quite innocent of the charge, I was summoned before a Court of Inquiry, to have this weighty matter investigated; when, by the statement of the gentlemen who were present at the time this improper expression was said to have been uttered, I was fully cleared from the imputation. The occurrence, however, was of service to me; as I learned, that had the epithet been used, however justly applied, the consequences to me would have been serious.

To return to the subject: among the Officers appointed to accompany this detachment, I was included,—and a very pleasant situation I was in truly: a march of about two hundred miles before me, no money in my purse, and about thirty pounds in debt to the tradesmen of the town;—but there was now no time to lose, and upon informing my creditors that they should be paid as soon as I arrived at my destination, they very kindly agreed to this arrangement. We set off the next morning, with only sixpence between my brother Sub and myself, which we shared in a glass of ale on the march, wishing each other better luck and more prudence in future. We trudged on, meditating and moralizing on our late extravagance; for in general it is only necessity that reminds us of our folly.

For the sake of some of my young military readers, I hope to be excused for pursuing this topic a little farther. On a young gentleman's joining a regiment, he is too apt to be dazzled by the new life of apparent pleasure that he is about to lead; but, if his fortune be limited, the greatest care and economy are requisite. The utmost circumspection, too, is required in his conduct, especially at the mess-table, where the want of politeness, good address, and propriety of speaking, on his first appearance, is often lastingly attended with the most unpleasant consequences. A deficiency in these qualifications will not fail to impress his associates with an unfavourable opinion of him; and according to the impression made, will he be subject to be treated till that impression is removed, which, in many instances, is not the case during the time of his remaining in the regiment. It may be supposed, that no gentlemen enter the Army without these previous acquirements; but admitting this to be the case, they cannot have that experience which their seniors have gained by long habits of military decorum and observation. It is, therefore, particularly displeasing to see these young men officious, talkative, presumptuous, and conceited, which, unfortunately, is too often the case. They should have the modesty, however clever they may be, to keep reserved; and for the first two or three years employ themselves in the study of men and manners, which they will find one of incalculable benefit. Be it observed, I am not one of those tyrants, who say that Subalterns should not be allowed even to think; nor do I mean to insinuate that they are not to join in the convivial conversation and merriment of the jovial companions with whom they associate: I only prescribe moderation and economy. Had I myself observed these prudent maxims on my entrance into the Army, I should not, at the time of which I am speaking, have found myself penniless; neither should I have fallen asleep on the highway from inebriety, and run the risk of being crushed to death by the wheel of a mail-coach.

"Chewing the cud of" not "sweet" but "bitter fancy," in this kind of meditation, we had arrived at our billets, when our ears were saluted by hearing our noble Captain order two courses, with plenty of wine, for dinner. It was now, indeed, that we blushed for our late prodigality, which, as marching-money was not then allowed, caused these orders to give us no small pain. We well knew that our late extravagance would not permit us to partake of the proposed cheer, and were obliged to explain to our commandant the state of our finances. The generous soul, instead of the conduct too common to pampered insignificance, when applied to on such occasions, sympathised with our feelings, and said, "Do not let that distress you, my boys; I will supply you with every necessary till we arrive at the end of our route, when you can take such means to reimburse me as may best suit your convenience." This kind and liberal act never can be obliterated from my memory. Indeed, a pleasanter march than this I never had, though I have experienced many a one since. Our route lay from Derby to Liverpool, where we embarked for Dublin, but were obliged to put into Amloch in Wales. We were treated there in the most friendly manner by the ancient Britons: more kindness and hospitality could not be shown to strangers than we met with; they vied with each other who should best entertain us—some with the lively dance, some with the melodious harp, while others made parties of hunting, coursing, and shooting. Here, too, I had an opportunity of visiting their extensive copper-mines, whose richness and novelty much delighted me.

In this agreeable harbour we remained wind-bound a fortnight; during which time the inhabitants not only continued their kind attention to the officers, but even sent potatoes and other vegetables on board, to the men, who were living on salt provisions, and in every respect afforded us all the comfort and attention in their power. Having left these good-natured people with regret, we reached the great city of Dublin, and in a few days marched for Cork. I could enlarge much on the occurrences of this journey; but, as almost every one is acquainted with travelling from one town in the United Kingdom to another, and the many incidents in general met with at the different stages, it would be uninteresting to enter minutely into details. Let it suffice to say, that on arriving at Cork, I found myself in the midst of my friends and relations, by whose means I was not only enabled to pay my kind benefactor his advances to me, but also to send back the amount of my debts to Derby, as I did not return to that place, having in the interim become effective in the first Battalion, then quartered in the barracks of Cork.

Behold me now, then, stationed where I receive every indulgence, and friendship; in short, I am quite at home. After adorning my person with plenty of powder and perfumes, along queue, and all the *etcetera* of military finery, away I strut to the grand parade, admiring the *belles* and the *bon-ton* of this gay place, and fancying myself equally admired, little dreaming how soon these fine ornaments would be tarnished, and the white powder exchanged for black, on a more arduous and active kind of service.

We remained here about four months, which were spent in one continual round of amusement,—balls, plays, assemblies, parties, &c. Indeed, a man may travel far before he meets with more hospitality than is to be found here. At length orders arrived to embark for England; and after taking an affectionate leave of all my friends, I sailed from Passage, and landed at Ramsgate, without any remarkable incident; a tedious passage and bad weather being mere common-place occurrences. We arrived safe at Deal barracks, where in a few days we received orders to embark on a secret expedition.

I must here beg leave to state, for the particular information of my younger military readers, the kind and soldier-like admonition of our brave Colonel, Sir George Smith, on this serious occasion. He convened a meeting of all the officers, and having politely and kindly congratulated us on the present undertaking, he thus addressed us: "Now, gentlemen, you are about to join a grand expedition; and if I mistake not, there is not one of you that has yet had the honour of seeing a shot fired from an enemy. It is therefore necessary to acquaint you that the whizzing of the balls is apt to cause a disagreeable sensation; but this, gentlemen, arises from a mistaken idea, for the moment you hear that sound, the danger is past. You will not, therefore, show a bad example to the men by ducking your heads and flinching your bodies, for that is unsoldier-like, and may cause a panic in the troops; but always keep the head up, the body erect, and even in danger show a pleasing and determined aspect, which may command respect and admiration in your men, and animate them to that glory which Britons have a right to anticipate." This salutary advice was lost on me at the time, for the duty of the heavy baggage being in dispute between another officer and myself, and decided in his favour, he consequently proceeded with the regiment; and I remained behind, and thus lost all the honours of the glorious siege of Copenhagen, where the very officer with whom this demur with regard to priority had taken place, and in whose identical situation I should have stood, holding the same colours, received his death-wound. This event I took much to heart at first, but after hearing his fate, I became more reconciled, and fancied myself reserved for greater undertakings.

In this I was not mistaken, nor was I long kept in suspense; for the regiment had scarcely returned to England, and again settled in Deal barracks, when it received the route for Portsmouth, to rendezvous there for another secret expedition, which was to be commanded by General Spencer. The destination we ultimately found to be Ceuta in Africa.

I was determined that no circumstances whatever should prevent my going on this occasion, so anxious was I to share the fortune of my brave comrades. We commenced our march, and soon arrived at the port of embarkation. Here was a new scene to me; an army of about ten thousand men, all busy in preparing and laying in stock for a long voyage: all appeared bustle and conjecture; however, after remaining here some time waiting for a fair wind, we set sail with a favourable breeze, which lasted just long enough to waft us into the swell of the Bay of Biscay, the name of which will ever cause my bosom to swell with horror: we were hardly in it, when the unpleasant command was given by the Master of the transport to take in sail. This was repeated again and again, till at length a storm stay-sail only was left standing. This was soon literally shivered to rags, and we were left to scud under bare poles. The storm now increased, and the density of the clouds became thicker and thicker, till it blew a most tremendous gale, which continued with little variation about ten days and nights. During this time, we were prevented obtaining either fire, or candlelight, and those who could eat were glad to make their Christmas dinner of cold junk and biscuit; but the troops had little occasion for any, their appetites being quite gone. Judge, then, the situation of one who had been so little at sea before; I cannot recollect half the dreadful sensations that seized me,—from the noise of pumps that were continually kept going, the different parts of the masts and rigging giving way, with the bustle and confusion of the crew endeavouring to work the vessel, and the great probability that we should founder, our ship having but just returned from a long voyage to South America, and being so much out of trim, that she was more fit to be taken into dock than to contend against a violent storm. In this plight our situation became each moment more dreadful, distress was depicted on every countenance; to look around, all was awfully sublime,—nothing to be seen but huge waves, on the tops of which we seemed like the inhabitants of the skies; then descending into the trough of the sea, we were as if entombed in the bottomless pit, never more to rise. Every swell seemed as if it would overwhelm our little bark; not a single ship was in sight, for the convoy had long since dispersed, many of them never again to meet, as they experienced that fate which we had every reason to expect. During the whole of the time we remained in this perilous state, the Master had not a single opportunity of taking an observation, as the sun never made its appearance: we could not, therefore, tell whither the storm was driving us. I am unable to give the reader the exact time this terrible tempest continued, for, never haying kept a journal, I am entirely indebted to my memory, which although not very strong, is nevertheless pretty correct, nor would I exaggerate intentionally, upon any consideration, one particular of this narrative. About the tenth day the Master was enabled to take an observation, and found us nearly in the latitude of Vigo. Indeed, we soon had proofs that he was accurate in his reckoning; for the sky had scarce begun to wear a milder aspect, the wind and waves to abate their fury, and the men to get a little respite from their fatigue, than we descried, bearing down upon us under a press of sail, a French lugger privateer, supposed to be from that port. Orders were instantly given to clear the deck for action, which were as instantaneously obeyed. In this dilemma, imagine to yourself a being like me, more dead than alive from sea-sickness, now ordered to get up and fight, and to set an example to the men by boarding from the bows. I certainly obeyed my orders to the best of my strength and ability, but must confess, I would rather have remained in my berth, had it not been for the honour of the thing; which, by the way, I could have well dispensed with at the time—such is the all-powerful effect of this terrible malady.

The troops, amounting to two hundred men, were directed to prime and load; the one half of them to lie concealed below, and the other to be ready on deck, a proportionate number having been allotted to assist in manning the guns, for we had carronades on board. During the time of these preparations, the enemy was fast coming up with us, and continually firing to bring us to; but we not complying, they ran along-side, and hailed us, asking what we were: the answer was, "A transport." They then asked where from, and whither bound. We informed them; and they, seeing us so well prepared to receive them, put their ship about and sheered off: on seeing this we fired one shot, which they did not think proper to return, but going right before the wind, were very soon out of sight. We were now just beginning to put things in order, and make ourselves a little more comfortable, the soldiers to commence cooking and cleaning themselves, the sailors to dry themselves, and repair the damage the Vessel had sustained, when another strange sail hove in sight, and of course the same preparations were necessary; but we were soon at ease on this head, as it was discovered to be one of our own fleet that had parted convoy, and, like ourselves, weathered out the storm, which, I must here observe, the greater part were not able to do, being compelled to put back into Falmouth harbour.

We had now arrived in a certain latitude, in which instructions were given to open our sealed orders. These directed us to rendezvous off the Rock of Lisbon, and we made that head-land in a few days. We were standing off and on there for some time waiting farther instructions, and had the pleasure of seeing the King of Portugal sail through our fleet, (which by this time had in part collected,) on his escape from the French to his Brazilian colonies, under the protection of Sir Sidney Smith. Fresh orders now arrived, instructing us to proceed to Gibraltar, for which place we immediately steered, and cast anchor in that Bay three days after. I received here the pleasing intelligence of my promotion to a Lieutenancy; but many, as you will find, were the storms and dangers I had to encounter previous to my obtaining farther promotion.

## Chapter 2

# To the Mediterranean

*See how the golden groves around me smile,*
*That shun the coast of Britain's stormy isle;*
*Or, when transplanted and preserved with care,*
*Curse the cold clime, and starve in northern air!*

*Here kindly warmth their mountain juice ferments*
*To nobler tastes and more exalted scents:*
*Ev'n the rough rocks with tender myrtles bloom,*
*And trodden weeds send out a rich perfume.*

Addison

On our arrival at this, the strongest garrison in the world, we were not permitted to land our troops, the fortress being already too full, and provisions exceedingly scarce; we therefore remained on board about three weeks, waiting the arrival of the rest of the convoy from England. During this time it came on to blow from the Eastward, which is here termed a Levanter: blow, indeed, it did, if possible, more hard than in the Bay of Biscay, and the havoc caused to the ships then at anchor here baffled all description; some cut their cables and tried to beat out to sea, many were jumbled together by means of their cables twisting, others had signals of distress flying, and minute-guns firing, but no one dared venture out to their assistance in this tempestuous sea. Amidst this confusion, to increase the scene of horror, night approached, and a small vessel came floating along-side our transport without a soul on board, as we afterwards found. The sentry hailed, and receiving no answer, according to orders fired into it; this was followed by others doing the same, supposing it to have been an enemy, sent among us from Algesiras by the Spaniards, who might have taken advantage of the gale for that purpose, as they were then at war with us: this circumstance gave the greatest alarm, and caused a brisk fire of musketry to be kept up for some minutes. From the darkness that now prevailed, no one knew the cause, but we were apprehensive that fire-ships had been sent among us by the enemy. This kept us on the alert the whole night, and the next morning such a spectacle of woe presented itself as is seldom witnessed: eleven fine ships, one a transport full of troops, all stranded, some gone to pieces, others lying on their beam-ends. An American trader, close alongside our vessel, drifted on the rocks, bilged, and went down; indeed, we could have thrown a biscuit on her from on board; and, had not the gale moderated after continuing three days, we must have inevitably shared her fate, as we had also drifted a great deal. At last it ceased, and an ill wind it is that blows nobody good, for, from the disaster of the unfortunate American, we derived much benefit, hauling up three pipes of fine Cape wine that floated along-side our ship, which was shared in regular daily proportions among the whole on board.

We remained in this disagreeable Bay three weeks, and saw no appearance of the rest of the convoy joining us. The communication of the garrison was shut in consequence of its neighbouring enemies, and there were no more provisions than were necessary for the troops stationed there, together with a deficiency of water; it was therefore found expedient to send us to Sicily, particularly as that island was at this time seriously threatened with an invasion by the French on the Calabrian coast. Orders were accordingly given to proceed: our sea-stock by this time being quite exhausted, we procured a fresh supply, which, though rather scanty from the dearth of the place, was in a great measure compensated by the many fine turtle we caught on the voyage. They were not, it is true, of the same species that an Alderman would like to partake of, yet we managed to make most delicious soup of them; and, instead of Madeira, took care to relish it with copious draughts of black-strap. The wind, which on our sailing had been fair, favoured us as far as Sardinia, into which kingdom we were obliged to put, owing to the breeze becoming adverse. We came to anchor in the Bay of Parma, where we were detained many days waiting a more favourable gale. During this period we spent our time in various pursuits—boating, fishing, visiting the country, &c.

Amusements of this kind, however pleasant they may appear, had nearly ended very disastrously to me. One day, accompanied by four others, I went to the farthest part of the island to shoot wild-pigeons: as soon as we reached the shore, which was very high land, we perceived the Blue Peter, which is the signal for sailing, hoisted; but, as we had frequently seen this flying many days before that event took place, we treated it very lightly, and pursued our sport, thinking we should have time to join the fleet previous to its departure. In this, however, we were much mistaken; for when we returned to the beach, our consternation was excited at seeing the convoy under weigh, and, to complete our embarrassment, the boat which conveyed us to land was not to be found. We had directed the boatman to go about a mile along-shore, at which place we intended to meet him; but having struck into the country, we could not direct our course exactly to the spot we wished, owing to the obstruction we met with from the great quantity of high myrtles and geraniums, which grew there as plentifully as our furze-bushes on waste lands: we now began to halloo, and fire our fowling-pieces, in hopes of making the boatman hear us; but to no purpose. Supposing, therefore, that he had gone off to the fleet, we held a Council of War, to decide whether we should go to the Martello Tower, at the extremity of the island, near which the ships would pass, and make signals to them for assistance, or proceed to the little village of Antioco, (to which I had been before, along with the Master of the transport, to purchase stock,) and endeavour to get a passage in one of their *feluccas* for Malta. We determined on the latter measure, taking care to keep along the shore in hopes of seeing our boat, which, after proceeding about half a mile, we had the good fortune to descry, making all sail to gain the ship; we lost no time in firing all our pieces together, and the man hearing them, directly put the boat back for us, and we reached the vessel just in time to save our passage.

That the reader may have a better idea of our unpleasant adventure, he must be informed that this is one of the most wild and savage-looking places imaginable. On our excursion, we met some of the inhabitants, and saw their habitations, into which they invited us to enter, asking in a kind of *lingua franca*—a language peculiar to the Mediterranean, whether we were French or English. From this circumstance you may form an idea of their ignorance; with respect to their barbarity, I can only judge from their appearance, not from their actions, for they were certainly very civil, and particularly assiduous in pointing out the places in which we were most likely to meet with different kinds of birds. But the figure and savage appearance of this race of mortals were truly original; their visages were dark, rough, and desperate; their make exceedingly athletic, and their dress nearly resembling that which Robinson Crusoe is represented to have worn, only that instead of having pistols in their girdles, they had a large stiletto on one side of their goat-skin jackets, which they wore with the fleecy side outwards, and a smaller one on the other. Besides these, they constantly carry a musket about six feet long, of a different kind from any I had seen before, the barrel being hardly large enough to admit the top of the fore-finger into the muzzle. They are in general mounted on very pretty little horses, which are here found in their wild state: they are extinct in all the other countries of Europe, but abound in the woods of Canais in the Island of Antioco. They are a very small race, exceedingly swift, and belong to whoever can catch them. I should imagine these people are so constantly armed from the fear of wild beasts, or more probably of the Barbary pirates, who frequently make a descent on these shores, and carry off every thing that comes within their reach.

I could not perceive much beauty in the women of this country, with the exception of their fine sparkling black eyes; their awkward dress, which was a short blue gown, very thick about the waist, and coming very little below their knee, prevented any judgment being formed of their make, but their feet were small and pretty. They appeared very industrious, and in the village of Antioco were all busily employed, in a manner that might prove advantageous to most cottage families in this kingdom. In every house, I observed a small mill placed in one corner of the room, in which they grind their corn: this machine was worked by a donkey, with very little trouble; they thus saved the expense of the miller, and were certain of getting their flour genuine, the benefit of which is obvious. Indeed, I never ate better, finer, or whiter bread in my life, but their meat was altogether as bad. On killing some sheep which we had brought on board, they were literally so poor, that when hung up, and a candle placed in their carcase, they were no bad substitute for a lantern.

This is not a neat village, being built very straggling; but the scenery about it is pretty enough, particularly as you look towards an old monastery which is entirely grown over by the prickly pear,—a plant very common in these Islands, which gives it much the appearance of the ivy-covered ruins so frequently to be met with in my own country.

From the singularity of this place, I am afraid I have been led to lengthen this description beyond my limits; I shall therefore conclude, by saying that their deportment was civil, though, from their terrific look, I have often blessed my good fortune in getting so well out of their power.

It being late at night when we reached the ship, I soon turned into my berth, and this, during the whole of the voyage, was on the cabin-floor; for, being the junior Subaltern on board, I was obliged to put up with the worst accommodation, it being in our profession, *semores priores*; but, bad as it was, I could not help fancying it a bed of down, in comparison to the one I should have got, had we been left behind in that deplorable and horrible place. It may be a fine country, and the inhabitants were certainly civil to us, yet it is deplorable, from the excessive poverty so prevalent along the shores of the Mediterranean, and

I say horrible, because I have still my suspicions with regard to their barbarity; and notwithstanding their courtesy to us, while our fleet was in the Bay, I should not like to trust myself with them unprotected.

The next morning was very fine, and we had just made the high land of Sicily, going at the rate of about four knots, when our Master, who had never been in this latitude before, observed the Commodore and other ships taking in sail, the cause of which he could not conjecture; but he soon found it out to his cost. I am not going to take up the reader's patience and time again with a tedious account of a long storm, a gale, a hurricane, or a Levanter; but merely to give you some idea of what is termed in these seas, a White Squall. It first made its appearance by a little white cloud, which became larger as it hastily approached, and in less than ten minutes burst upon us with a most tremendous roar, like the whizzing and exploding of a bomb. It proved fortunate that we were in the rotten state before described, from a previous long voyage; for, had the sails been of new canvass, nothing could have saved us from being capsized. Luckily as it was, they were shivered into a thousand pieces, and we lay on our beam-ends for some minutes, in such a situation as I cannot describe, but I observed every soul clinging in the greatest dismay to every thing that could be laid hold of. This state of apprehension was exceedingly awful, for we feared that the vessel would not recover herself; happily she soon righted again, and in about ten minutes all was as calm and serene as if nothing had happened, and the only remaining vestiges of the squall were, the deck being covered ankle-deep with hail-stones of an enormous size, and the tattered appearance of our sails. From the great damage that we in particular had sustained, the whole convoy were obliged to put into Palermo to refit, and we now again experienced the good effects of an ill wind, for it gave us the opportunity of seeing this beautiful city, while the sight of us was equally gratifying to the inhabitants, as they never, I believe, had before seen British soldiers there, and were much in want of them, from the apprehended invasion.

We remained here about three weeks, and took every opportunity of seeing the most noted edifices and curiosities of this great city and its vicinity. The buildings here are very fine; and so are the public gardens, which are laid out in most delightful walks, shaded by cypress, citrons, myrtles, jessamines, and geraniums, interspersed with elegant fountains, the most fragrant groves, and shady bowers. Here you may seek a retreat from the rays of the sun, and, reclining at your ease, observe the verdant balmy avenues, promenaded by the most lovely women. Indeed, the very air of this sweet spot seemed to breathe that soft voluptuousness of feeling, that can create none other but the most tender passions, which indeed are here cherished in the fondest degree. If the fair Eve had a paradise like this, how she could commit a deadly sin, I cannot conceive!

In company with some brother officers, I went in a hackney-chariot, of which there are a great number, as in London, for the accommodation of the public, to visit Montral, a small town at a short distance, and which has the finest church I ever saw. I do not recollect to what Saint it is dedicated, but it is distinguished by noble architecture, fine statuary, superb pillars inlaid with mosaic to the very top, and representing various kinds of figures, paintings by the greatest masters, and altar-pieces of the finest porphyry, adorned by the richest sculpture representing Scriptural subjects. Here are also the most valuable relics of religion; and the structure is likewise endowed with costly gifts of jewels, pearls, and all kinds of precious treasure; in short, such is its magnificence, that I can only regret my inability to do justice to it in description. The situation is as elevated as the fabric is grand, and on our way to it we were continually winding up a steep ascent, which gave us a most delightful view of the city and bay below, with our fleet at anchor; but this was surpassed by the country around, which was for the most part composed of plantations of orange-groves, interspersed with olives; indeed, so plentiful was the former fruit, that the country-people ate it with bread as our peasants do cheese. Even the little children on the road ran after our carriage with small branches of this tree, containing four or five fine oranges in a cluster, in hopes of receiving a few halfpence: these oranges, when cut in two, produced a juice as red as the coats on our backs, from being engrafted on the pomegranate-tree, and they are certainly the finest species of this kind of fruit in Europe.

We every day came on shore to enjoy the fine walks, the grand prospects, and the amusements of this fascinating place, on which Art and Nature have been so profuse in lavishing their beauties, the whole of which we were only prevented from enjoying, by Fortune not being quite so bountiful in the embellishment of our purses.

It was with great regret we were obliged to quit this charming town and all its fascinations, but it is rarely the fate of a soldier to remain long in one place. We proceeded to Messina, where we landed, and marched the same day into the interior, so that we had not an opportunity of seeing much of that great city, but in passing through it, observed that it had suffered much from the convulsions of Nature: and so exceedingly subject is this place to earthquakes, that we felt a severe shock of one during the time we lay along-side the quay, which agitated the water so as to occasion great motion to be felt in our ship; but the natives appeared to regard the phenomenon with much unconcern.

Our road was here truly romantic: we had many glens and vales to pass, and precipices and mountains to ascend, one of which struck us all with consternation; for, on arriving at the summit, it appeared as if it had been cleft asunder; and in reality so it had: I suppose, by one of those tremendous shocks so frequent in this country. The opening was about fifteen feet wide, and so deep that the bottom could not be seen; it appeared as if the earth had yawned with wide-extended jaws to receive us into her bowels. This gulf we were compelled to cross by files, by means of a plank placed across, and a rope on one side to steady us; only one could pass at a time, from the apparent flimsy construction of this bridge, over which, however, the mountaineers ran with the greatest indifference. Passing this defile as fast as the encumbrance of our accoutrements would permit, we soon reached our quarters, which were in pretty villages, dispersed over the heights of this singularly diversified country.

Our men, after being so long at sea, now began to find themselves very comfortable, and asked for a little money to add to their happiness; when, although I gave them only the value of one sixpence each, to my great surprise, on visiting their rooms, I found them all completely intoxicated, the wine being here so exceedingly strong and cheap,—about one penny per bottle: this circumstance made me more cautious in future how I distributed their pay.

The village in which I was quartered was named Jesso, and a most excellent billet I had. My habitation was a very large monastery, part of which was allotted to the men, and the remainder occupied by a great number of jolly fat Friars: indeed, I may well call them such, for they gave me one of their cells with a bed, crucifix, beads, and every apparatus similar to their own; and every evening,. on returning from the mess, I received a constant visit from the Abbot, with a bottle of excellent wine in one hand, and a plate of fine fruit in the other, the produce of his own vineyard: over this we used in general to sit and talk, although he knew not a word of English but "Long live King George de Third," nor I one word of Italian but *"Bono vino, Signor."* Another great advantage I had in this cloister was the romantic and delightful view from the window of my cell; for, independent of the most picturesque *coup d'oeil* of every thing that could be found in rural scenery, was Mount Etna throwing out clouds of smoke on the one side; and on the other, in the midst of the sea, Mount Stromboli vomiting a perpetual torrent of flame. This last phenomenon being at so great a distance, appeared to me like a light-house well lighted; and it was perhaps intended as such by nature, to caution the wandering mariner against the dreaded rocks of Scylla and Charybdis.

In this agreeable society time passed pleasantly enough; but the duty was rather severe, as our picquets had to descend a great distance to gain the beach, where it was conjectured a landing might be attempted. This descent was easily effected;

but it took us some hours to return, owing to the difficulty of re-ascending these precipices, which were rendered very slippery by the wet weather. We were now ordered to retrace our route to Messina, there to re-embark and proceed to Syracuse. In the spacious harbour of that place, (for a finer, I suppose, there is not in the universe,) we remained at anchor about a month, disembarking our men daily to exercise: this duty finished, we amused ourselves by visiting this now small town, once the emporium of the world. It even yet bears evident marks of its once towering grandeur, in the mouldering ruins, scattered in ponderous heaps over an immense space. In my perambulations about this ancient town and its environs, my attention was continually engaged by the amazing masses of grand antiquity that presented themselves; "the gorgeous palaces, the solemn temples"—all dwindled away. Among these I observed the pillars of Jupiter Olympus, which have at present the appearance of two columns, such as might be met with in some old abbey in my own country.

I then visited the fountain of Alpheus and Arethusa, where I was informed I should find the most beautiful nymphs bathing: and so I did; but they were in the shape of smart young washerwomen, with their petticoats tucked up far beyond their knees, scrubbing their linen. The baths, which have still the remains of grandeur, are now the receptacle of all kinds of filth.

I next went in company with several others to see the cave of Dionysius, where that tyrant used to confine all persons suspected of treason. This horrible and extensive cavern was cut out of a solid rock, in the shape of a man's ear, with a tube at the end, communicating with a secret chamber, in which this king used to sit and listen to the conversation of the prisoners below; and if any of them displeased him by their discourse, he directly ordered them to be decapitated in his presence. To this secret chamber there is now no access but by means of a rope, slung through a pulley, at the bottom of which is tied a piece of wood. Across this the curious put their legs, and are thus drawn up to a height of about two hundred feet. On this slight conductor, one of my companions got across, with the intention of being drawn up a little way, and after that let down again. Having gone about twenty yards, he called out lustily to be let down; but the Sicilians mistaking this for his anxiety to go faster, pulled with greater velocity, and he soon arrived at the secret chamber, where there was a man stationed to haul him in,—after which they let off some *patararas* in the cave below, which made a roaring louder than the loudest thunder. The difficulty was now to get him down, which was effected by the guide above tying a handkerchief round the waist of our adventurer and the rope, by which method he was lowered in perfect safety. There were some naval gentlemen looking on, who were used to rope exercise, but they would not venture up,—so perilous did this expedition appear. Indeed, we were all quite satisfied by the description our friend gave of it, without going through the same aerial exploit. We next went to view the Amphitheatres, some of which were nearly perfect: they gave us a good idea, from their spaciousness, of the immense number of spectators that must have assembled together, to witness the gladiators and public tournaments, when in the zenith of their glory; but, in their present state, they only reminded us of the gradual rise and rapid fall of the most flourishing cities of antiquity.

From these remains we walked to pay our respects to the inhabitants of the regions of the dead,—a kind of sepulchre under their churches. Here we saw thousands of their forefathers, who had not been in existence for many centuries, all standing upright, by means of wires by which they are suspended, and in great preservation, having gone through a certain process of embalming, something, I should suppose, in the manner of the Egyptian mummies. It was very remarkable that in this awful abode there was not the least disagreeable smell; but the physiognomy of some of the figures was horribly ghastly,—a circumstance plainly distinguishable by the burning of several lamps: indeed, the scene was not calculated to gratify any other feeling than that of curiosity. These receptacles of the dead are visited once a year by the relatives of the deceased, who kiss them, bow to them, kneel to them, and pray for them, and show them every respect, as if they were alive.

Our next visit was to the catacombs,—another habitation of those who have long since departed this life. These are subterraneous vaults, cut out of the rock, of such an amazing extent that the termination is not now to be found. In the passages niches are cut, in which the bodies are placed as if in a coffin; they are most wonderful undertakings, and show what care and trouble the ancients must have taken for the accommodation and preservation of their dead: indeed, we might almost imagine that they paid more respect to their deceased parents, in former times, than the present generation do to their living relations.

The various relics of antiquity in this place are so numerous, that I must refer my readers to the more interesting pages of Bridone, for a full and correct description of this beautiful and curious island. Mine is not a book of travels, but is intended merely to give an idea of the variety of scenes which those who embrace the profession of arms are likely to witness.

Before quitting the subject of this enchanting country, I cannot refrain mentioning the very moderate price of provisions here. My friends may recollect, when I first entered into military life, I was spending more than double my pay; in this island I could not make away with one half of it, for it only cost me one shilling a day for my messing,—indeed, I could have lived on my rations (for which I paid twopence halfpenny only), being allowed a pint of good wine per day, besides bread and meat; but I chose to pay the above sum for the delicacies of the season.

At length we received orders to quit Sicily, and reluctantly set sail for Cadiz, to join the other part of the expedition, which had proceeded to that port, and had not for a length of time known what bad become of us. On our way we touched at Malta, where we came to anchor for the night; but had not time to see this strong fortress, except from the offing: it appeared to be wonderfully fortified. The next morning we got under weigh, favoured by a gentle breeze; and nothing more than plain sailing occurred during our passage, except that one night, as we were going pleasantly before the wind, every one snug in his berth but myself, being with the watch on deck, we perceived a large ship close on our stern, which the mate hailed, and desired to keep off; but hardly were the words out of his mouth, when down she came upon us with a most tremendous crash. In an instant the commanding officer and all hands were upon deck, in their undressed state, to know what was the matter, supposing we had struck on a rock and were going to find a watery grave. Of course the first person the Commandant called for was the officer of the watch; on perceiving me, he saluted me with, "God help me! God help me, Sir! what is the cause of all this commotion?"

I related the particulars to him, which convinced him that no blame attached to us; and, observing that I was busy with the men on duty in assisting to get clear of our unwelcome visitor, he soon returned to his warm berth again. The case was very different with our poor little doctor, who was the greatest sufferer; for his berth being near the stern, where there was a large utensil, which be in general contrived to keep pretty full, this was unfortunately broken to pieces, and the contents nearly smothered the poor little man, who, as he appeared on deck in this shivering plight, was the cause of affording us much mirth. He, however, soon retired to shift his night-robes, and change his resting-place to a drier corner.

This accident was very severe, and caused our vessel considerable damage,—smashed the skiff, stove in. her stern, carried away the main chains, and otherwise materially injured her.

Soon after this occurrence we made the rock of Gibraltar: we took in a small supply of water, and stood on for Cadiz, where we arrived the next day, and joined our expedition after being separated more than three months. We were received with great pleasure by our old acquaintances, who, while they were in harbour, pitied our unfortunate fate, thinking our rotten transport could not have outlived the length and fury of that outrageous storm. However, I consider we had by far the best of it;

as I should have been sorry to have exchanged the opportunity of seeing the Mediterranean Islands, particularly that kingdom which was once esteemed the garden of the world, for their view of Falmouth.

## Chapter 3
# The Battle of Vimiera

*Wide o'er th' ensanguined field, with carnage strewn,*
*In horrid triumph Death exulting strode;*
*And piteous was the sight of slaughter there,*
*And thrilling were the groans of agony.*
*But soon the warrior in the battle-field.*
*Becomes familiar with these scenes of blood;*
*By duty lesson'd, and by custom taught,*
*Their horrors views with unaverted eye,*
*Though still of feeling soul—nor less humane*
*Than he, with sinews yet unused to war,*
*Who would turn pale, and sicken at the sight.*

Penrose

The bustle and gaiety of this fine town, although in a state of bombardment by the French fleet at the time, afforded us considerable amusement and pleasure during our continuance; for here, indeed, gaiety itself appeared attended by all the Graces, in the lovely persons of the Spanish ladies, who, after their *siesta*,[1] promenaded the public walks (the shot from the enemy not reaching farther than the suburbs) in the greatest crowds, and with the most stately and graceful deportment. It is a pity my fair country-women have not an opportunity of imitating their majestic carriage, which is the only acquisition in which these pretty brunettes have the advantage; for with respect to every

1. A sleep after dinner—a general custom in Spain.

other grace and virtue, no nation in the universe can possibly claim the pre-eminence.

The attack upon Ceuta having been abandoned, in consequence of the dispersion of the fleet, and other affairs of greater moment demanding our exertions, our troops were, for the present, to be disembarked at Santa Maria, on the opposite side, where we remained very comfortably situated for about three weeks; but the weather was so excessively hot that we were obliged to exercise in the night, and sleep during the meridian heat,—a heat, indeed, so intense, that the Spaniards have a proverb, which says, that only Englishmen and dogs are to be seen in the streets at that time.

We now received orders to embark and join our great chief, Sir Arthur Wellesley, who subsequently so conspicuously distinguished himself in the late glorious war. This intelligence gave me the greatest joy; I was now in hopes of gaining some of those laurels of which I was deprived on the expedition to Copenhagen. We sailed, and reached Portugal before the army had commenced its march, and landed at Figueras with as little delay as possible, but with the greatest difficulty, owing to a most tremendous high surf, in which the inhabitants were obliged to come naked and take the men from the boats, to prevent their ammunition from being wet: this was attended with some danger, several of the boats being swamped. Having landed without any serious accident, after a long and tiresome march, for the most part up to our ankles in sand, we came into camp with the grand army that evening.

I was rather premature, when I remarked, on my first joining the regiment, that then began my life as a soldier: I had hitherto partaken more of that of a sailor—now indeed was the martial life commenced, and that too in the most irksome manner; the fatigues of which are probably more severely felt by those moving in the situation of Subalterns, than by any others. Many of those officers, I am persuaded, did they please to dedicate a little time to the illustration of the active part of their career, would accumulate honour for themselves, and benefit their profession. Indeed, had I the just pretensions belonging to many of my friends who have served in these campaigns, delicacy would prevail over my inclinations also, and I should rather attempt to smother than mention my services, fearing a narration of them might appear like ostentation or egotism. But as they are trifling in comparison with what most of my military readers have met with, I am under no such apprehension, particularly as I am aware that the life of a Subaltern, however imperfectly told, will, if replete with greater incident, be read by a generous public with greater interest, than that of a Field Marshal. But to resume the thread of my narrative. On our arrival in camp, the first thing done was to select the officers and men for duty; this railing on me, I was instantly placed on the quarter-guard, stationed on the top of a hill which commanded an extensive view of all approach to the camp. Here was my couch for the night—a great contrast to the snug warm berth I had been used to on my marine excursion: indeed, I now began to wish I had made choice of the Navy for my profession, from its greater apparent advantages.

We did not halt long here; for the enemy being in the immediate neighbourhood, and hovering about us in every direction, it was found necessary to proceed to active operations; for which purpose we had previous directions to land in light marching order,—that is, with not more than one man can carry on his back. My kit consisted of only two shirts, two pair of stockings, and other little necessaries in my haversack, with a great coat, and three days' provisions,—which, however, was a very fatiguing load in this hot climate: the. men are of course more burdened, but then they are from infancy more inured to hardships, and proportionally better able to bear the inclemency of the weather, and the fatigues and privations incident to war, than those who are nursed in the lap of luxury, which, unfortunately for me, had been my lot in the early part of my life; and I had been rendered almost too delicate for this hardy service, by the over-anxiety and care of too fond a mother.

Before entering upon the account of my first campaign, I

think it necessary to observe, that were I to mention every particular occurrence—the state of the weather, the number of leagues of each day's march and counter-march, for the thousands of miles I travelled the country, almost incessantly for the space of six years, with the names of the different halting-places, and the daily duty which is usually performed, it would swell this work to an endless extent, and would render it quite insipid from the constant and unavoidable repetitions. I shall therefore give the reader a general idea of our daily route, which was commonly observed throughout the whole of our operations, by giving a condensed view of one day's march, and can afterwards repeat any extraordinary journey, should I find it necessary for the better elucidating of different events.

One day's march,—The route having been received, the drum beats at any hour of the day or night, as occasion may require, to assemble the troops—I cannot gay in all cases to strike the tents, for in this campaign we had none. After the Adjutant has collected the reports, the troops move off in as large divisions as the nature of the road will permit to march commodiously, encountering the dust or the rain, the heat or the cold, the mountain or the valley, as the climate or the country may chance to present, till they arrive at the ground on which they are to bivouac for the night. Here, after piling arms, parties are sent out under the superintendence of a Subaltern to fetch water, others to draw rations, some to cut wood both for fuel and to build huts, while others are selected for guard, piquet, foraging, and other duties. This being done, fires are lighted, and (should the utensils have arrived) cooking commences. After getting a scanty meal, a parade is formed, to see that the men have cleaned themselves and their accoutrements, in readiness for the next day's march, and that they have their necessaries, particularly their ammunition, complete. This daily routine of duty being performed, the soldier is glad to lie down soon after on his bed of fern, straw, or, if nothing else is to be had, to repose his wearied limbs on that cold bed which will eventually receive him into its bosom. Being now entirely equipped for our ensuing campaign—having provided bill-hooks, camp-kettles, and mules for carrying them, with baggage-horses and every other convenience, we broke up camp to prosecute our active duties, and continued marching till we came up with the enemy, who had taken an amazingly strong position on the heights of Rolessa, from which, after marching four leagues that day, we had to attack and dislodge them. Measures being accordingly taken, by executing such manoeuvres as would bring us in contact with the foe—having previously fixed bayonets, primed and loaded, &c. we drew nearer and nearer to the scene of action. It was now that I could have dispensed with the honours of a military life; and had it been as honourable to have gone to the rear as to the front, I should certainly have preferred the former, and that in double quick time; for whatever heroes may say, yet to me I must confess it caused a little imperceptible tremor, notwithstanding the brave and manly admonitions of Sir George. I was, however, fully convinced of the truth of his assertions; therefore, stifling this sensation, I soon found that spirit which I imbibed from my ancestors take possession of my heart, and which, thank God! never forsook me in the hour of danger.

We now began to advance over those who had fallen: among them was my brother Sub, who had been out skirmishing; and we came under what I then thought a pretty hot fire, both of field-pieces and musketry, not having witnessed the like before: but this I found was a mere joke to what I was hereafter to experience. However, it gave me a seasoning—as I was soon after knocked down by a musket-ball striking me on the left groin; and I only attribute escaping a severe wound to having some papers in the pocket of my pantaloons, which prevented its penetrating the flesh; but it caused a great contusion: I was, however, in a few minutes able to proceed with the regiment, and soon had the pleasure of seeing the French flying before us. We followed them till the lateness of the evening compelled us to halt, when, this being the first field of glory I had the honour of sharing in, I could not help noticing immediately at my feet a fine youth who was shot through some vital part. This poor soldier, when I first observed him, was lying on his back, his head. supported by his knapsack: his visage appeared serene and calm, with a very healthy ruddy colour in his manly cheeks; but every time I looked at him, I perceived his countenance gradually becoming paler, and his fine blue eyes losing their lustre, which I observed soon became fixed in death, without his uttering a groan or a struggle.

From reflecting on this mournful spectacle, I was soon diverted, by being ordered to go on the out-post of a Field-officer's piquet, about two miles in advance. I went accordingly, and took my station behind a furze-hedge, from which I could hear the French videttes talk as plainly as I now hear the passengers under my window.

I was now, for the first time, on an out-post before the enemy; no covering but my great coat—no pillow but my cocked hat. The fine ornaments which had shone so conspicuously on the parades on home service, began to lose their brilliancy: the glittering epaulette was crushed into a thousand forms, and the pretty tight boot cut with many a slit to ease the blistered foot. Most glad was I to feel the morning sun warm my dewy limbs; and, hardly had it made its appearance, when we were called in, and had but just time to get a little warm tea, so refreshing to the weary frame, when off we marched in pursuit of the enemy, whom we followed up for a few days, till we reached the field of Vimiera, where we halted some time.

About nine o'clock on the morning of the third day, we perceived the French in great force on the heights of Torres-Vedras, coming down upon us, formed in strong divisions, and in the most regular array. We quickly stood to our arms, and marched to our alarm-posts, which soon brought the contending bodies in contact; when, forming line with the 71st Regiment, which had been engaged some time previously, we came in for our share of the conflict of that day, by being opposed to a strong French regiment, which advanced to within half pistol-shot of us, when a most tremendous point blank fire ensued. This not proving effectual, Charge! was the word now vociferated from flank to centre: but, on their seeing us come to this awful position of destruction in the art of war, they had not courage to withstand our impetuous movement; for, just as we were in the act of crossing bayonets, to the right-about they went, in the quickest time. We followed as rapidly, driving them from their artillery—I believe, about twelve field-pieces, passing it on the right flank at the same time the 71st Regiment did on the left, and I trust we had an equal share in the honour of capturing them.

The French, however, having now gained possession of the village on the heights, which had been strongly barricaded, remained there for the present, and we received orders to halt in the ravine. Indeed, a little breathing-time had become very necessary, as we had for the last two hours been firing, shouting, running, swearing, sweating, and huzzaing.

On the ground was found General Brenier, concealed in the rushes: he had been wounded in the leg and was now taken prisoner, and brought to our surgeon to dress. On cutting off his boot, we were surprised to see he had no stockings on; on this being observed to him, he very coolly replied, *"Le soldat Francais n'a pas besoin de bas."* From this place we were ordered to make a retrograde movement, as a *ruse de guerre*; which had the desired effect of enticing the enemy to rally. Having thus drawn them to a sufficient distance from their fastnesses, we came to our proper front, and gave them such a reception that they again ran off, and took possession of their stronghold, whence we soon had the pleasure of seeing the gallant Riflemen completely drive them. It was near this spot that I saw, as we advanced, a Scotch piper of the 71st Regiment lying on the ground wounded. This, however, did not prevent his cheering his comrades on to glory with their national music. They certainly are a brave people: but, as to their being more so than their neighbours, I never saw any thing in them as men or soldiers to make me think that they were.

We were not allowed to pursue the enemy farther than this village, being informed that we had done enough for that day. Why we were not permitted to do more, when we had it in our power, I am at a loss to conjecture—it is best known to those who were there and held a higher command. It is not my province to comment on the conduct or orders of my superiors in rank—I am now merely recording what occurred to myself: and this reminds me of my levity previous to the engagement; for, in general being blessed with a good flow of spirits, and making it a rule to put on the best face I was able on every unpleasant occasion, even were it only for example, I was laughing and joking, when one of my brother officers came to me, with his visage very much cast down, being unwell at the time, and remarked that I ought to be thinking of something more serious at that critical moment He observed that many a fine fellow would soon be laid low, and sent to the next world; adding, that he had a presentiment that something fatal would that day happen to himself. The poor fellow, in about ten minutes after, received a cannon-ball in his neck, which almost severed his head from his body. Another occurrence happened, previous to our line advancing, to my brother Sub, which had nearly terminated in a similar manner. He was very near-sighted, and the French artillery playing on us at some distance, the unevenness of the ground made the balls come hopping similar to those bowled at cricket, which caused the men to open right and left to let them pass: at one of these openings this officer stood, and addressing himself to me, asked what was the matter? I replied," Do not you see what is coming?" at the same time giving him a hard pull I was the means of saving him from that sudden death the other had just experienced; however, taking his quizzing-glass to his assistance, he gladly observed the ball pass about one hundred yards to his rear.

When this day's fight was over, those who had escaped had congratulated each other on their good fortune. Amongst these was an officer who had his hat much shattered by the splinter of a shell, which a junior one perceiving, said—"Oh, my dear fellow, I am very sorry to see your hat so broken!"

"Thank you," replied the other, "but I suppose you would rather have seen my head, and then you would have risen a step."

We now returned to our former ground, and immediately fell to work making fires to boil our kettle; for, though the killed and wounded presented shocking sights on all sides, this did not take away our appetites: the more habitual a distressing scene becomes, the less it is regarded, till at length such sights are rendered familiar.

We went to sleep on this bed of honour with as much unconcern as if it had been on soft and downy beds at home, hoping that the morning's dawn would lead us on to a rapid pursuit. As usual, one hour before daylight we stood to our arms: but, to our astonishment, we received no orders to follow the enemy. I well recollect the observation of every individual—"What keeps us here after so complete a victory? Why do we not advance and overtake the foe?" No one could tell—all was conjecture and amazement, tin we were at length informed of the well-known Convention of Cintra, which put an end to this campaign.

## Chapter 4
# Corunna & Beyond

*Convention is the dwarfish demon styled,*
*That foil'd the Knights in Marialva's dome,*
*And turn'd a nation's short-lived joy to gloom.*
*Here folly dash'd to earth the victor's plume,*
*And policy regain'd what arms had lost.*

Byron

An armistice now took place, and such terms having been agreed on between the chiefs of the two contending armies as enabled the French to abandon the kingdom without farther molestation, we continued a leisurely march to Lisbon. After about three days, we halted in a most delightful spot, in the midst of vineyards, olives, and orange-groves. My comrade and myself set about constructing our little hut, and pitched upon a hollow piece of ground for that purpose. This slight shelter merely consisted of a few green branches, to screen ns from the scorching rays of the sun and the dews of the night. A finer evening than this there could not be; and at dusk we stretched ourselves on our bed, made of fine soft rushes, which grew here in great abundance. We had enjoyed the blessings of a sound repose but little more than an hour, when we were awakened by peals of thunder breaking over our heads; these became more loud and dreadful the nearer they approached, until the whole earth seemed to tremble. The thunder was accompanied by vivid flashes of lightning, followed, in a few minutes, by the most impetuous torrents of rain. Our snug settlement in the ravine was very quickly covered with a rapid stream, in which, by the constant light of the electric fluid, we perceived all our loose articles of dress, the only part we had taken off, such as shoes, hats, sashes, belts, &c., all floating away, and we had great difficulty in saving them. So heavy did the rain fall, that it ran down the boughs of our hut like as many small water-spouts pouring upon us; and we found it more eligible to stand out in the midst of it, than to remain in the occupation of the hut. Nor was this the worst part of the business; for I had unfortunately been very unwell, even before the campaign commenced, but feared to acknowledge it, lest it might occasion my being left in the rear and deprived of the honours of it. As soon as the morn appeared, and the rain had ceased, we dried ourselves, by collecting all the huts together and setting them on fire, and then continued our march to Caliboose, where the army went into camp for some weeks. I proceeded to Lisbon on duty, where I saw the French army embarking for France, on board the very transports that brought us to this country, agreeably to the late Convention. An extraordinary sight it was; for they had their standards displayed in the square of Belem, with as much sangfroid as if they had been the victorious army, and had dictated the agreements. Indeed, they seemed to have some reason for considering themselves so, from the terms they made; for they embarked with their heavy baggage, (I should rather say plunder,) their arms, horses, and artillery, with colours flying, drums beating, bayonets fixed, &c.

Immediately after the evacuation of Lisbon by the French, our regiment received orders to march into the city, and was quartered in the citadel. This capital has so often been described by its numerous visitors, that I shall content myself with observing, that I thought it most remarkable for its excessive filth; it is not, however, without its advantages. In this city we remained about a month, enjoying all the amusements of a town life; but in the midst of these pleasures, the route again came to embark and sail for Oporto. We had a very pleasant passage; but it is not my intention again to enter into the particulars of a sea-voyage, which could only have the effect of tiring and perplexing those who have patience to peruse these common occurrences.

On our arrival off the harbour of Oporto, we found that there was not sufficient water to take us over the bar, so that we were obliged to take to our boats, and land among the rocks. In doing this, there was great danger, from the prodigious swell and exceeding high surf which constantly prevail here, and render the presence of skilful pilots necessary in landing troops. These, when what they call the master-wave made its appearance, gave a signal to us with their hats, waiting for which we lay upon our oars. As soon as they made the motion, the Portuguese boatmen, who were well acquainted with the business, pulled away with such surprising quickness, that, from the exactness of the time which they kept, it was more like clockwork than manual labour, and the swell, with their dexterity, generally carried the boat high and dry on shore. I was told, that had this not been the case, the next wave would inevitably have swamped the boat: this, however, did not happen in a single instance during our disembarkation; so well do these men understand this kind of navigation.

On our landing, we marched into the fine and friendly city of Oporto; and a most excellent, generous, and hospitable town we found it. We were here shown the greatest attention possible: I never heard men or officers complain of their billets, so accommodating were the inhabitants in consequence of the great intercourse between this place and England. Indeed, speaking from my own experience, I have ever met with more condescension, respect, kindness, and favours from foreigners, even in an enemy's country, than I have hitherto found in my own: with them, in the hour of need, have I shared the frugal repast of the peasant, and the more sumptuous entertainment of the *grandee*.

From this benevolent town we marched to join the army under the command of Sir John Moore. I accompanied my regiment as far as Lamego, where, being taken seriously ill, I was left with orders to take charge of, and, as soon as I was able, to bring on a detachment of convalescents; so that, though sick, I was still on duty.

In the mean time my illness increased to such a degree, that my life was despaired of by the Portuguese; and I have since been informed that their priests were about to administer extreme unction to me. Considering all hopes of recovery over, they went through this solemn ceremony peculiar to their religion; and having thus, as they thought, sent my soul to migrate quietly to another world, it was not deemed necessary to give me any more medical aid or nutriment in this mortal state. They even objected to my servants rendering me any longer the only assistance I could obtain; for this town not being at that time a sick depot, no surgeon of our own was to be had. My servant communicated this strange proceeding to au officer who was detained in the town; and this gentleman, by means of an interpreter, begged they would leave me to my fate, stating that I was not of the Catholic religion, and that my servant would do every thing necessary for me, whether I lived or died. He also desired that he might be allowed to pay me every attention.

In a few days after this event a favourable crisis occurred; and in about three weeks I was able to proceed with the detachment to my regiment, which had joined the troops under Sir John Moore. This being the winter season, I marched with my party a most fatiguing route, in the worst of weather, and over miserable roads, through dreary woody mountains, interspersed with wretched villages, inhabited by the most deplorable objects of poverty and filth I ever beheld; in fact, misery appeared to be the only visible object of the day. So very offensive was it to enter these repulsive abodes, that we should have much preferred remaining outside, had it not been for the inclemency of this severe and wintry season.

We had proceeded some distance beyond Almeida, and within a few days' march of the army, when we were met by an express, informing us that the French had reached Astorga, and consequently had cut us off from Sir John Moore, who was now in full retreat. We therefore joined that part of his army who were, like ourselves, cut off; consisting of several entire regiments, with various detachments. In fact, this was part of General Moore's troops, retrograding on a different line of march, encountering the similar wet weather, equally bad roads, the same if not greater distance, and probably more privations, than any other part of his army,—having no Commissary with us, and being obliged to retrace our steps through cork and chestnut forests, which were in many places rendered impassable from swamps and quagmires. The country, too, had been so continually ransacked, that poverty, wretchedness, filth, and disease, only were to be met with. Every thing that could be got at had already been destroyed by the enemy, and Desolation had laid her withering hand on all within her grasp. In this deplorable state of affairs, I was compelled to endure such unusual hardships, immediately on getting the better of my late illness, that I was brought to a very low condition, and obliged to crave assistance even from these unhappy peasants, into whose huts I was often driven from weakness, fatigue, and hunger. In these dwellings of sorrow have I frequently begged the scanty meal of boiled chestnuts, which these poor people cheerfully gave me. This fruit is, indeed, their principal food; the woods in these parts abound with it: the poor people gather the chestnuts in the season, and preserve them for winter store. They are prepared much in the same manner as potatoes are in Ireland, and are eaten with salt.

On our return to Lamego, we embarked in boats, and went down the Douro to Oporto. Owing to the rapidity of the current, we arrived the next day,—a distance of about one hundred and fifty miles. On this passage we overtook a boat which had just preceded ours, but had unfortunately struck on a hidden rock, and upset. We passed it, keel uppermost; and the day after we saw about two hundred dead bodies floating in all directions,—there being very few out of more than two hundred that embarked, including women and children, that were saved.

Thus I again arrived in this city; but, from the fatigue and harassing duty I had lately endured, I was not in the same state of health as when I left it. Hardships had brought on a relapse of illness; and from the constant hurry and confusion, I had not had an opportunity of changing my linen,—so that on my arrival at Oporto I was literally swarming with the worst description of vermin. In this state the physician of the forces visited me, and finding me labouring under a severe rheumatic fever, he ordered me to be removed to another billet. By great good fortune I got into such quarters, in point of grandeur, as I had never before met with, in the mansion of a Portuguese *fidalgo* or *grandee*. Here was an immediate change from absolute wretchedness to the height of magnificence: but a few hours before, I was either exposed in an open boat to the rain and the rapidity of a dangerous current, or perishing in the thick woods; now, I was housed in a superb palace, decorated with the most splendid chandeliers, beautiful mirrors, and costly furniture. As soon as I entered, my noble and worthy host came to pay his respects, and appeared to sympathise in my miseries. He requested to know my wants; I informed him all I then wished for, in my weak state of health, was to retire to rest. A sumptuous apartment was immediately prepared, where I slept very comfortably, and found myself much refreshed; having been provided with clean linen, while that which I had on was thrown off and committed to the flames, previous to my taking possession of my grand bedchamber!

The next morning the butler came to know what I chose for breakfast, and I informed him my physician had prescribed milk diet. He then went away, and soon sent a servant, in a rich livery, carrying an urn of gold upon a salver of the same metal; I had only to turn this reservoir into a beautiful china basin, when it was instantly filled with the richest milk. All this appeared like enchantment, when but a day or two previous I was getting my scanty repast on the high road, and my bed in some old pillaged church, deserted house, or open field; I could not help fancying that the ancestors of this wealthy man must have been companions of Pizarro, Gonzalvo, Cortez, or some of those adventurers to the New World, and had gained these immense riches from the spoils of the innocent natives. My breakfast being finished, my *patrone* paid me a morning visit, when he requested to know whether I would dine with his family or by myself: I preferred the latter, in consequence of my illness. He also invited me to take an airing in one of his carriages, which I refused for the same reason. He then took his leave; and soon after came the steward with a bill of fare, to know what I would choose for dinner, and whether I would please to have it cooked by a French cook, or by their own. I, partly out of compliment, preferred their own cookery, with the exception of garlic, which they commonly introduce most profusely into their dishes, and to which luxury I afterwards became quite reconciled. He desired me to name the wine I chose to drink; but this indulgence I was obliged to decline, not being allowed to live so high.

The same etiquette was observed daily; the time passed very pleasantly, and I found myself improving in health very fast. I had a fine library for my amusement, and a beautiful garden for my recreation, intersected by most delightful walks and transparent fountains, in the basins of which sported multitudes of the finny tribe, variegated with the most beautiful gold and silvery hues, as if they partook of their owner's riches: here were also delightful groves and bowers, formed by plantations of orange, lemon, and of jessamine trees, woodbines, and various other fragrant shrubs.

In this enviable state of comfort I remained but a short time, for it is not a soldier's fate to be allowed a long indulgence in the peaceful enjoyment of social happiness. I had only been in this hospitable and magnificent abode about three weeks, when one morning my noble *patrone* came to my bed-side, with a woeful countenance, and said, *"Ah Senhor! Senhor!"* he then paused awhile, and with tears trickling down his aged but good-natured and manly visage, proceeded to inform me that he had just received certain intelligence of the French army, which had so recently driven the English into the sea at Corunna, being now under the command of Marshal Soult, within three days' march of this city.

This unwelcome news was in a few minutes confirmed by my servant bringing me the orderly book, in which I had the mortification of seeing orders for the British troops, then in the town, to march to Lisbon, and the sick to embark on board a transport in this port, for the same place. Now the enchantment was broken: every one was in bustle and confusion; some flying with their goods and chattels into the interior of the country, there to hide themselves in the mountains; others trying to secrete their wealth from the rapacious grasp of that overwhelming host which was now about to pour down upon them.

After taking a grateful farewell of my kind benefactor, I went on board, and we had nearly suffered a great misfortune: for as we were in a very large ship, there was not water sufficient to take her over the bar, and we were delayed another day. The French being now within one day's march, every countenance wore the appearance of despair; we could not get over by the evening's tide, but determined, even contrary to the advice of the pilot, to make a dash at all events the next morning. It soon arrived, and the advance-guard of the enemy were now seen on the neighbouring heights: we cut our cables, and struck with great violence on the bar; but fortunately the succeeding swell carried us clear out to sea, and on our arrival at Lisbon we learned that the French had entered immediately after we had quitted the Douro, which made us not a little pleased at our narrow escape from being made prisoners by them.

We here formed a junction with the other troops, for all the regiments and detachments that had been cut off from joining the northern army were ordered to rendezvous at this place; and here, from our great numbers, we were formed into battalions, called the first and second battalion of detachments, which composed a very fine body of men. I was attached to the latter. We remained waiting reinforcements about six weeks, which appeared to me a long time, not having been so long in one place for the last two years. I suppose the same struck our commanders, as we were desired immediately to re-equip ourselves in complete marching order, and be in readiness to move at a moment's notice. The moment soon came, and a strong body of troops having arrived from England, we left our cantonments at Lamere, in the vicinity of this town, and again took the field, to commence a more arduous and glorious campaign.

## Chapter 5
# The Battle of Talavera

*By Heaven! it is a splendid sight to see*
*(For one who hath no friend, no brother there)*
*Their rival scarfs of rich embroidery—*
*Their various arms that glitter in the air!*
*What gallant war-hounds rouse them from their lair,*
*And gnash their fangs, loud yelling for the prey!*
*All join the chase, but few the triumph share;*
*The grave shall bear the chiefest prize away,*
*And havoc scarce for joy can number their array.*

Byron

We commenced our march for Oporto, to which spot our line of operations was directed; and had only been on our route about four days, when to our great joy we were overtaken by our former General, Sir Arthur Wellesley, who came to re-assume the command. I well remember with what enthusiastic huzzas we cheered him as he passed our line of march; the men from that moment, as if by instinct, wore the countenance of confidence, which never forsook our army even to the conclusion of the contest. We halted a few days at Coimbra, to be reviewed, and a very *tight little* army it was; such a one as was soon to make these legions of boasting Invincible[1] fly, who had, as they termed it, driven the English into the sea at Corunna.

1. Previous to the taking of Oporto, they really fancied themselves Invincibles; for though they were fairly beaten out of the field at Vimiera, yet, from the advantageous Convention they made at that place, they considered themselves victors.

On the march to Oporto, with what pleasure and satisfaction, as we moved tediously along the road, did I think of revenge on those fellows who had so recently broken the enchantment of my princely residence, and endangered my liberty on the bar of that port! The time was fast approaching, when I was to experience the same pleasure that they had enjoyed on entering the town,—that of seeing them fly in all haste, with the addition of leaving the greater part of their plunder, baggage, artillery, and many prisoners, behind them. On this march we halted a few days at Alhobaca, in whose hospitable monastery the friars entertained us in the most sumptuous and friendly manner. In this religious and spacious mansion, I sat down to dinner with about three hundred officers: they accommodated us in the grand saloon, with their Padre, who appeared to be a venerable, good, and agreeable man, at the head of the principal table. I am told that this monastery had been granted thirty thousand dollars yearly to entertain all travellers, of whatever nation; but the French have since burnt this magnificent and benevolent institution to the ground.

As we approached nearer to the banks of the Douro, every step brought us into scenes more horrid. The enemy's advanced posts had in these parts left numerous marks of their ravages, and traces of their skirmishing. We now began to see the dying and the dead: some of these had been mangled in a manner too shocking to be described, by the Portuguese female peasants, out of revenge for the brutal treatment previously experienced from them. Now we passed clusters of inhabitants hanging mutilated on one tree, and on the next as many French were suspended, all hacked and gored in the same manner, by way of retaliation; such was the animosity subsisting between these inveterate foes! The priests were busily employed in taking down their unfortunate countrymen, praying for them, and burying them.

Having at length reached the banks of the Douro, we perceived the enemy in great numbers in the town of Oporto, which they had partially fortified, and had destroyed the bridge to prevent our crossing. This did not daunt the energy of our

Commander, or the courage of his troops; we were directly ordered to take to our boats, and after a severe conflict the enemy were driven from their guns, and the town soon after taken possession of. It was with the greatest difficulty that the Duke of Dalmatia and his staff escaped: and so sudden and successful was the attack, that they had not time to sit down to the dinner which had been prepared for them; but, quitting the place with precipitation, left this good cheer to the conquerors, who so much better deserved it. My wishes now became realized by this glorious triumph. I had now the satisfaction of seeing the foe run helter-skelter away as fast as their legs would carry them; the streets were strewed with their dead, which the inhabitants allowed to remain a few days in a naked state, as a mark of scorn and derision,—a conduct which the French had entailed on themselves by the atrocities they had committed in this unfortunate town.

But it still remains for me to describe one of the most melancholy tales of woe.—We halted here the next day for a supply of provisions, of which we were much in want, while the light division of the army followed up the enemy; and I took this opportunity of paying my good old *patrone* a congratulatory visit on the expulsion of the French. My astonishment may be more easily conceived than described, when, on arriving at the scene of my late happiness, I found nothing but bare walls remaining. The house had been completely stripped of all its costly furniture and every thing that was valuable, by the desperate robbers who were now flying before us. To witness the destruction occasioned in this beautiful residence was truly pitiable: on entering, I perceived the fine balustrades broken; the chandeliers and mirrors were shattered to pieces; all the portable furniture had been taken away, and the remainder either wantonly burned, or otherwise destroyed; the choice pictures were defaced, and the walls more resembled a French barrack than the abode of a Portuguese *Fidalgo*, from the obscene paintings that were daubed upon them. The beautiful garden was entirely ransacked; the charming walks and fragrant bowers torn up and demolished: the fountains broken to pieces; and the crystal-like water drained off to catch the little fish, I suppose to satisfy the wanton appetites of these all-devouring marauders. However, I was somewhat relieved from my apprehension and sorrow on the account of this worthy family, by being informed that they had made their escape to England, in a vessel of their own, at the time we sailed, with all their plate, money, and most valuable property.

While here, I went to visit a Welsh gentleman who had married a Portuguese lady. He was a resident of this town, on whom I had been billeted on our first landing here, and from whose family I received much attention, but had been unable to wait on them on my last arrival, owing to indisposition. He was not living at the same house, but I was directed where I might find him. My interview with him proved of the most painful description: he met me on the stairs, and received me with great kindness, but appeared in a very dejected state of mind. He showed me into the parlour; and, pointing to an arm-chair, told me that in that seat a French officer had, a few hours before, blown out the brains of his poor old father-in-law, because he would not resign one of his daughters to gratify the abominable lust of this detestable assassin, who suspected she was secreted in the house, though in reality she had fled to the mountains on the first approach of the enemy. There was no corroboration of this shocking catastrophe necessary, as the blood and parts of the skull were still visible in the chamber, but the body had been removed. His amiable wife, from whom I had received the greatest civility, and whom I wished to congratulate on the liberation of their town from such vile miscreants, to my regret could not make her appearance; she was too much overwhelmed with grief. My friend was about to enter into the particulars of his misfortunes, occasioned by the arbitrary contributions and severities of the French, when the drum beat for us to fall in, and continue the pursuit of the routed army. On taking my leave of him, he squeezed me by the hand, offering up at the same time his fervent prayers, that we might soon overtake these execrable murderers. These sights I merely mention as having come under my own observation, and as specimens of what must have been the general atrocities, bad state of discipline, and insubordination of the French troops, under the command of their blood-thirsty leaders. We pursued the enemy night and day, barely taking sufficient rest to support nature, till we came to the frontiers of Spain, taking a great many prisoners, baggage, and commissariat stores. At length, finding themselves so hardly pressed, and not being able to make another stand, they were compelled to take to the mountains, and disperse in all directions, which rendered it impossible for a regular army to follow them any farther.

We had no sooner dispersed these legions, than our indefatigable Commander-in-chief received information of another French army, under the command of Marshal Jourdan, being concentrated in the neighbourhood of Madrid. To this part we were ordered instantly to direct our route,—an exceedingly severe trial for troops who for the last four months had been incessantly harassed, and were now in the greatest want of every article of dress, shoes in particular, and of almost every comfort of life. The very moment in which we thought we should have rest, by ending the campaign in the dispersion of the French, brought the orders to continue a march with little intermission of about five hundred miles. Yet not a murmur was heard on this critical occasion; for what will not British soldiers perform under a brave and victorious general? We retraced our steps in the first instance from Chaves, a frontier town, towards Oporto, the roads being excessively bad, and the weather very showery, as it was the commencement of spring. A few days after we passed through the fine town of Braga, but owing to the intricacies of the roads in this unknown part of the country we penetrated into a forest, where they narrowed into unbeaten tracks. There we became benighted, and very short of rations, which obliged us to provide in the best manner we could for ourselves, till the bugle assembled us at daybreak. Straying about this wet and miry spot, being too cold to sleep, I at last saw a light at some distance, and I made towards it. I found that it proceeded from a large deserted farm-house; for this situation being near the borders, was more open to the country. On entering the house, I found a large fire, around which were many soldiers occupied in picking fowls, which they had purloined; and before it hung several half-picked that were roasting; some of the party, more fatigued, lay sleeping about till the repast was ready. Having warmed and dried myself, I had the good fortune to get some tea made, (a little of which we in general carried in our pockets, as the baggage, owing to impediments, was frequently two or three days' march in the rear,) and ate a leg of a fowl, which one of the men gave me, but without any bread with it. After this refreshment, I laid myself down on a mattress, the covering of which had been taken away. Here I got a sound but short nap, and waking in the morning, I fancied there was something uncommon under me, as the mattress felt hard and uneven: on looking, I found, to the agreeable surprise of myself and the men, who observed they wished they had had it last night with the fowls, four immense flat loaves of yellow *pong*, a kind of bread made of Indian corn, well known to the troops by the above name,—quantities of this grain growing here. This bread is very sweet and wholesome; it resembles pound-cake very much, and constitutes the principal food of the inhabitants in this part of Portugal.

Continuing our long and difficult route, we again arrived at Oporto; through which town we proceeded without any' delay. One circumstance I ought to notice, which was pointed out to me on passing,—this was, a large opening in the wall, on the inside of a building out of which the French had taken upwards of 100,000 doubloons, about £300,000 English money. There is no doubt that they must have had private information of the treasure, as the wall had been plastered up so completely, after it had been deposited, that no eye could possibly have discovered the hoard.

We now trudged on over a vast extent of country: into the toils and difficulties of this route I shall not enter minutely, as

I have already given a general outline of one day's march. Perseverance at length brought us to Abrantes, about the centre of Portugal; here we rendezvoused for about three weeks, to give the whole army time to concentrate and re-equip, and to afford an opportunity for the fresh troops from England, then on their march from Lisbon, to join us. This being accomplished, we prepared to leave this fine encampment for the heart of Spain: I call it a fine encampment because we had had time to build our huts with neatness, regularity, and strength; they were thatched with boughs, had chimneys, were railed in, and formed into regular streets, which gave them the appearance of a fine green village.

Being provided with necessaries, and proper arrangements being made, we broke up camp, and soon arrived at Placentia, where we halted a few days. This was certainly a most oppressive situation: in Portugal we had experienced the most distressing cold and wet weather; it was now as suddenly become as intensely hot, and we had very little except the olive-trees, which we were prohibited from cutting, to screen us from the scorching rays of a sun almost vertical. This being an open corn country, we were the whole day exposed to its beams, and the ground was so exceedingly warm, that it produced the greatest number of insects I ever saw. We were infested and annoyed, beyond measure, by the scorpions and centipedes crawling over us, and the mosquitoes stinging us in such a manner, that I have frequently seen officers and men with their eyes so swollen that they could not see out of them for some hours. In the day we sometimes amused ourselves by catching these scorpions, which we did by turning up a large stone, under which there were in general two of these little animals nestled together; then throwing a thread with a noose in it over them, and touching them at the same time with a straw, they would instantly dart their long tails over their heads to sting; and by drawing the noose tight we caught them alive, and hung them on a tree as a punishment for their nightly depredations. They are very venomous visitors; one of our men lost his eye from their sting, and many others were much hurt by them.

Our advance continued, and the weather retained its sultry heat. Many a weary step, over many a dreary league, we dragged through the dusty way; sometimes not seeing a house for days together, sometimes without a drop of water to wet the parched and swollen tongue of the way-dropped soldier—for there were many who sunk under the oppression of this excessive heat. We had frequently no fuel, not even a shrub that would serve as a piquet for the baggage-horse; and occasionally no forage was to be had for these poor animals after their hard day's labour, in which case they had to move on till they came to a more verdant spot. However, as our commissariat had hitherto procured us plentiful supplies, and we received our rations very regularly, we were enabled to continue our exertions till we arrived at Talavera de la Reyna.

Here we halted some time; when, about the third day, as we had just commenced cooking, the drum beat to arms, and we distinctly heard the advanced division under General M'Kenzie,. who so gloriously fell there, severely engaged. We seized the meat, half-cooked as it was, out of the camp-kettles, and putting it into our haversacks, marched off, and arrived at the position just in time to receive the enemy. They experienced a pretty hot reception from our British soldiers, who were a handful in comparison of their numerous battalions; for it was well ascertained that they had from forty to fifty thousand men, while the British had barely nineteen drawn up in line. This line their legions made repeated efforts to break, attacking our flank, centre, and flank, and flank and centre again; but with very little effect. The engagement commenced about four in the afternoon; and towards midnight there was a general cessation of fire, as if by mutual consent, each army appearing to wish a respite from this destructive carnage. During this short pause, by the light of the bright moon, reclining on their arms, the expectant warriors stood, sanguine for the renewal of the fight; ere dawn of day, the dreadful roar of all-destructive cannon again commenced, and a fresh attack ensued even more spirited than the former. It was a most tremendous day; such a continual clash of arms, incessant fire of musketry, balls whizzing, and shells exploding, that I am at a loss to describe the consternation, yet sublimity of this great battle.

I must here observe, that, although we had so small a number of the British, there were about thirty thousand of our allies, the Spaniards, in line with us; but they were mere ciphers on the occasion, being neither attacked nor engaged during the conflict. My battalion being on the right of the line, nearly joining theirs, I could plainly observe their actions; they certainly fired, but I could not perceive what they fired at, nor did I afterwards see many of their troops dead on the field, out of about fifteen thousand that shared that fate.

Night now began again to draw her sable veil between these murderous hosts of mortals; the musketry again ceased, but only as it were to increase the roar of cannon. We were now under a most tremendous fire of shot and shells; but luckily our flank only being exposed to it, they fell in every direction about us without doing material mischief.

By this time I became much exhausted for want of food; for the meat that we had taken half-cooked with us, had, from the heat, become so full of animalcule, that I could eat but little of it; I therefore gave it to the man next me, who, not being quite so nice, gobbled it up in a moment. Bread, however, was out of the question, and water only to be procured by going into greater danger. In this state, as we were resting on our arms, notwithstanding the roar of cannon, I fell fast asleep for an hour or two as soundly as if I had reclined on the softest couch. The dawn re-appeared, and one of the men roused me from my slumber, which indeed he had some trouble in doing. The cannonading had ceased, and we again stood to our arms, expecting another attack; but it appeared the enemy had got enough of it; for they, as we afterwards found, had moved off the ground, taking care to leave their advanced sentries to the very last moment. These were constantly calling out *Qui vive*? and making a great noise, to make us believe that the enemy were still there; but, as they did not come on to renew the contest, our light troops were sent out to reconnoitre; when they found that the French, under cover of the night, had taken the opportunity of retreating from the scene of action, leaving us masters of this hard-fought field. We then heard at intervals a few shots, and learned that they proceeded from the Spaniards, who were shooting the wounded French. There was in consequence an officer and twenty men from each brigade immediately sent out, to protect and gather together the wounded enemy; and I was one on this duty. I had only gone about one hundred yards, when one of my men, who were scattered for the purpose, called out for me to go to him, and told me that a Spaniard, whom he pointed out, was about to shoot a Frenchman, badly wounded; who was crying most piteously, *"Mon Dieu! Mon Dieu!"*

I waited to see what were really the Spaniard's intentions: he deliberately loaded his piece, and was going to present it at this unfortunate creature, when I arrested his arm, and sent him away; but, on looking behind me, I observed him creeping through the vineyard to return and accomplish the diabolical and cowardly act of killing a fallen enemy in cool blood! On seeing this I ordered my men to take the wounded man and remove him from the spot where he was, to some shady olive-trees, with which this plain was planted; and there I formed a kind of depot for these poor suffering wretches, with a guard to protect them till the carts came to take them away.

This was a most unpleasant duty: the scenes of horror I here witnessed, I cannot, nor do I wish minutely to describe; but one circumstance I cannot help noticing. On passing the ravine where the contest had been most severe, I perceived that a quantity of high sere grass which grew there had taken fire from the wadding of the guns; and the poor fellows who had fallen there, wounded and deprived of the power of escape, were literally burnt to death; which gave them all the appearance of pigs that had been roasted. A huge desperate-looking bravado of a Spaniard, passing at the time, drew his sabre, and deliberately plunged it into the body of one of these dead Frenchmen, who could now be distinguished only by their earrings, as the English and French lay here in mixed numbers, with their clothes entirely consumed. He then, pulling it out, all reeking with gore, triumphantly made use of a common Spanish expression, not proper here to mention, looking, at the same time, ferociously at me. I certainly thought his conduct most dastardly; but, on cool reflection, imagined that his motive was probably revenge. He might have had his wife torn from his arms, his family contaminated, his house burned, and his property destroyed; or, possibly, the same causes to seek satisfaction as my unfortunate friends at Oporto: yet, even under such circumstances, I could not help thinking it poor and paltry revenge to take such useless satisfaction.

Whatever sensations this gory scene might have caused to a reflecting mind, I must confess my own was engrossed by thoughts of a more interested nature; for having had nothing for the last two days, except one biscuit per man, and the piece of meat I have just mentioned, hunger became the most predominate feeling. I in vain searched among the dying and the dead, in hopes of finding some food to eat; but, if they had had any, it had already been taken by the men on duty and the Spaniards; all I could see that strewed the field, besides their apparel and accoutrements, was an immense number of *billet doux*, for which the French are so famous. For these, however, I had at this time very little relish, as they were a poor substitute for food. On this disagreeable duty I was strolling about, when I met an officer on the staff whom I knew; and telling him my situation, he shared with me a piece of bread, which he luckily had with him, and a little wine from his canteen, mixed with water, which had now become plentiful, the river, before occupied by the enemy, being free of access. This refreshment was a most seasonable and opportune relief, and I returned to my battalion, when I laid myself down to sleep; and, owing to the two last days' fatigue, I did not wake till we stood to our arms at daybreak.

This day we were in hopes of the arrival of the Commissariat, who we expected would have stuck to us in the hour of danger, and given us our rations. If meat was wanting, they might have given us bread, or biscuit, or, at any rate, they might have issued out wine or spirits; but, I am sorry to say, no provisions were yet delivered to us. I will not attach blame to that useful department, because I know not what was the cause of this omission; but this I do know, that we were the sufferers, and if the French had possessed the resolution to have attacked us another day, they would probably have penetrated our lines, not from their physical strength or courage, but owing to our exhausted condition, occasioned in a great measure by the want of these common necessaries of life.

The day after the battle came, and we received a pint of wheat a man; the following day the same; and the next, if I recollect right, the same. This supply, scanty as it might have appeared to those who were partaking of the roast-beef of Old England, with us, who were partaking in its glory, was as satisfying to the craving appetite, as mock-turtle to the pampered cit; for being boiled up with a little chocolate, it assumed a similar colour, and, what was more pleasing, it answered the same end. I cannot here omit a saying which one of the soldiers made use of on this occasion; which was: "They have given us corn today; I suppose they will give us hay tomorrow."

We remained some days on this field of putrid honour, if I may be permitted such an expression. In feet, it was literally and truly so; for the foetid stench that proceeded from the spot, was, from the heat of the weather, rendered intolerable. Indeed, the system of warfare appeared entirely changed; at the onset we used to bury our dead, but it now became more common to let them variegate the field with their bleaching bones.

At this period a most shocking spectacle took place. In consequence of many of the Spanish soldiers having run away during the action, twenty-seven of these unfortunate men, who had been taken, were tried by courts-martial, and sentenced to be shot. They were placed rank-entire on the battle-field, already strewed with dead bodies, and the priests having confessed and absolved them, the fatal word was given to a company of their own countrymen, drawn up for the purpose, to fire; and in an instant these poor wretches lay prostrate, adding to the dreadful slaughter, already too great, and affording a melancholy example to the cowardly.

About the fourth day, we received orders to move. Much has been said of the retreat from Talavera; but at this time there was no such thing in contemplation—at least as far as I could judge. We moved to the rear, it is true; but this rear had now become our front: and the intention of the movement was to meet another army which was rapidly advancing upon us, under the command of Marshal Soult, whom we had so recently put to the route, and dispersed in the mountains to the north of Oporto. He had again collected his forces, to the number of twenty thousand, and was marching in this direction to attack us; and he had already reached Placentia, when the intelligence arrived at our headquarters.

Our great and provident General, taking his measures accordingly, left the Spanish army, which had suffered but little in the engagement, to keep possession of the field of battle, and protect our sick and wounded in the hospitals at Talavera from falling into the hands of the enemy; the force of our allies being quite adequate in point of numbers to have stopped the progress of the French, in the event of their again advancing; the former having still nearly thirty thousand men on the position, and the enemy being reduced to about the same number. We, therefore, left this glorious, though terrible and sadly offensive field, and counter-marched for Placentia, being fully persuaded, from the valour of the Spaniards, of the security of our poor wounded comrades, who were previously comfortably lodged in hospitals, and not, as I have heard erroneously represented, abandoned by the British army.

Having taken up our ground for the night at Orapesa, a little town about a day's march from Talavera, we began to boil our kettles, and make dumplings with the flour that was this day delivered to us in lieu of bread; when we perceived the Spanish army, in whom we had placed such confidence, in full retreat, and close at our heels: and to this dastardly conduct alone is the abandonment of our unfortunate wounded to be attributed, as well as the necessity of our commencing a retreat.

This was the moment that the great discipline of British troops shone conspicuous—this was the moment that talents and generalship were to be displayed:—a powerful enemy advancing both in front and rear; the Spanish army in confusion, and no confidence to be placed in them; and provisions not to be had, as the French had cut off our principal supplies. These circumstances, together with the heat of the weather and the forced and harassing marches, rendered the state of affairs truly critical. In this dilemma, the most prompt and judicious plans were necessary; and such it will be seen in the sequel were adopted by our brave and noble Commander.

Our advance being, by these circumstances, converted into a retreat, the plan of operations was consequently altered. We proceeded towards the southern frontiers of Portugal, which being, I believe, a track never before pursued by British troops, led us completely out of the way of our depots and commissariat stores. We were, therefore, compelled to provision ourselves in the best manner we were able; but the all-wise Providence, in whom we trusted, never forsakes the brave, or the counsels of the just, when acting in a good and righteous cause.

This season of the year was exceedingly fine, in the midst of harvest—but excessively hot. However, we had plenty of forage for our cattle, which kept up our baggage. Mine was lost in the confusion of the battle of Talavera, but I was afterwards amply remunerated for it by the liberality of Government.

The mention of harvest, reminds me of an occurrence of the second day's march on the retreat.—Being entirely destitute of provisions, and halting in a field of wheat in the sheaf, our cattle living on clover, and we on air; they being turned into one, and we into the other; my servant, Thomas Standfast, and myself, set our wits, which were well sharpened by hunger, to work. I undertook the task of rubbing out the corn from the ears, and he took one of the horses to go and seek what he could find; in about an hour he returned, with little success, so many being on the same errand, and brought only some ripe mulberries. However, these mixed with the corn and some milk, which a goat that I had caught in the mountains gave me, and boiled up together, afforded us a most delicious repast, much resembling the furmety which I got when at school at Marlow; nor did I, over this meal, envy the sumptuous banquet of the most profuse gourmand. Indeed, our principal employment, at this time, after the march, was to invent new modes of satisfying hunger; as the Commissariat, in these days, thought nothing of letting us shift for ourselves for two or three weeks together.

Under these distressing circumstances, we were proceeding in as quick time as large bodies can well move, getting for the next fortnight nothing but goats' flesh, which we commonly collected and drove from the mountains, either on, or after the march. In feet, so hard were we now pressed for provisions, that I hope I am not incorrect in saying, we had permission to forage for every article that came under that denomination.

The march now became still more harassing, as our brigade brought up the rear, which was closely followed by the enemy till we passed the bridge of Arza-Bispo. In its neighbourhood we remained three days, to get the cannon up a steep mountain; this fatiguing duty came to our turn twice a day, to enter on which we had to wade through a river waist high,—a very pleasant employment truly, on not very full stomachs! however, by attaching about fifty men with ropes to each gun, besides oxen, we accomplished this work, with indefatigable labour, in the time above specified.

During our halt here, as some of our men were prowling about, seeking wild honey, goats, or any thing they could find to satisfy their wants, they by chance discovered, secreted in the cavity of a rock, about five hundred pairs of Spanish shoes, and a great many sacks of flour, which were most seasonably divided,—the shoes among those who were most in need of them, many being now entirely destitute; and the flour equally among the brigade.

On my returning late, one evening, from this duty, I found

the troops had crossed the river, which agreeably prevented my re-crossing that night; and the next morning, on rising from our bed of shingles, we continued our route, having previously destroyed all the useless lumber that could not be brought away. The enemy all this time looked down upon us from the opposite hills, neither attacking, nor following us farther than this place, having had a sufficient example of their temerity on the bloody field of Talavera.

Proceeding by easy marches—the weather still very hot, and extremely fine—affairs appeared to wear a more cheerful aspect, and every day's journey brought us into a more fertile and friendly country. We bivouacked in the environs of Truxillo, a very fine town in which is the mansion of Pizarro, the conqueror of America, which was now our head-quarters. Adjoining this, stood the small house of his father; who, I am informed, was a cobbler in this place, though afterwards enriched by his son's good fortune. Curiosity led my comrade and myself to visit these buildings, as we had heard that they abounded with the choicest rarities of the new world. Having seen most of the apartments, we were just about quitting them, when the Commander-in-chief himself arrived, and inquired our business there; and on being informed it was merely curiosity, he politely desired us to continue our researches.

Pursuing our now leisurely retreat, we passed through a most delightful and luxuriant country, abounding with pleasant villages and towns; among which may be mentioned, particularly, Merida and Medelin. Oxen are here employed, in general, to tread out the corn, there being no barns to house or thresh it in.

There was now no want of supplies, the Commissary having joined us; and every thing bore the appearance of content. We were in a plentiful country, and continued our route till we reached the well-fortified town of Badajos, and went into camp in the wood of Albuquerque, which ended this campaign. It was found necessary—in consequence of our having been in the country upwards of two years constantly on the alert, and without an opportunity of getting other regimentals than those in which we first landed, and which were now in a most tattered state—to proceed on to Lisbon; no trifling distance! However, not to be too prolix in my details, I shall concentre the ensuing chapter in the account of one night's adventure.

## Chapter 6
# A Night Adventure

*Je traversal je ne sais combien de champs et de bruyères, et sautant tons les fossés que je trouvais sur mon passage, j'arrivai enfin auprès d'une foret. J'allais m'y jetter, lorsque deux hommes à cheval s'offrirent teut-à-coup au-devant de mes pas.*

Gil Blas

*One night's adventure on the road to Lisbon.*—We now had nearly terminated the march, and halted for the night within six leagues of the banks of the Tagus, when some circumstance obliged me to proceed this distance, about thirty English miles, alone. I must observe, that this is one of the most noted places in Portugal for all that is dismal, dreary, and forlorn—wide extended heaths, immense forests, murdering *banditti*, &c. to increase my pleasant anticipations, we had previously been talking about the numerous murders and robberies committed in this neighbourhood; which, even by a good fireside, and snugly seated at our dinner, sounded sufficiently frightful and terrific.

About seven in the evening, I left the battalion to go on particular duty. I mounted my horse, having now made myself master of one by the fortune of war, and set off. I had proceeded about a league over the heath when night closed over me, rendered more gloomy by the wild-looking waste around. I fancied myself, like Gil Bias, made captive by the marauders who infest these wilds, dragged into a cavern, and perhaps doomed to servility under another Dame Leonardo. Other thoughts likewise intruded, which created ideas still more horrid. While I indulged in such meditations, a wolf, a wild boar, a large dog, or some such animal, I could not distinguish which, rushed from the brakes; but at all events it kept dogging me for about a mile. Sometimes it darted across the road near my horse's head; at other times, I could perceive it lurking behind me: at length, I lost it altogether. Proceeding a few miles farther, with my mind still absorbed by unpleasant intrusions of the imagination, my horse all of a sudden made a dead stop, and I saw something very tall and white, apparently in the middle of the road. It had the resemblance, from what I could discern by the light of the stars, of a tall person in a white garment; but to guess what it really was, puzzled me as much as it did my horse: indeed, I was much of his opinion, being more inclined to go back, than to face this direful ghost-like-looking object before us; but there was no alternative:—I had nearly completed half my journey; it was about the hour of midnight, and, recollecting that delay is in general the harbinger of danger, I again applied the spurs to my Cavallo, and made him approach a little nearer; the moon, at this moment bursting forth in great splendour from behind a dark cloud, discovered most fully to my view this terrible, ghastly-looking monster, in its real form—that of a beautiful white marble monument, which, by the inscription on it, I could discern had been erected in this lonely spot to the memory of a merchant, who had been murdered here by *banditti*: it did not, however, stand in the middle of the road, as I had first imagined, but by the roadside. This silent tomb did not at all tend to elevate my spirits, and I thought it prudent, in case of accidents, to proceed at a slower pace than before, lest by going faster I should knock up my horse, which had been on the previous day's march, and was in low condition.

I now approached the environs of a dismal-looking forest. The trees were stripped of their leaves; the moon shone very bright, and the branches being moved by a gentle breeze, and their shadows on the ground in constant motion, had the appearance of living objects, showing themselves in all manner of shapes and forms. In passing through this wood, I saw at some distance four or five horses tied to a tree, ready accoutred, and as many men lying on the ground. From my imagination being on the stretch, I conceived them to be *banditti* in reality; accordingly, I grasped my sword, not having pistols with me, but recollecting that there was little to be expected from its protection, and not wishing to appear hostilely inclined, I let it remain in its scabbard; and as I had no choice but that of going forward, I drew nearer, and called out to them. They answered in English, which certainly gave me some satisfaction; I inquired who they were, and was informed, a Quarter-master's baggage benighted, who had gone on in the day to procure billets. I proceeded a few miles farther, and arrived at an old house in this forest—the only one I had hitherto seen, and at which, as my horse and myself were much jaded, I was inclined to stop, and the poor animal seemed quite to concur with me, being very loath to pass it; but I had been informed in my previous conversation with my brother officers, that this was the haunt of nightly adventurers. I saw here no kind glimmer of light, nor indeed any friendly appearance—nothing of that look of cheerfulness and content, which might tempt the way-worn traveller to stop and seek refreshment; on the contrary, it had a very different aspect, somewhat wild and appalling: nor did it appear to be inhabited. I gladly left behind me this dismal retreat, into which I have no doubt many a weary passenger had been dragged by these freebooters, and never heard of more, being sacrificed to the rapacious views of the desperate ruffians.

I had now approached the skirts of the forest, and perceived, at a distance, two men mounted on excellent horses. The nearer they drew towards me, the more terrific was their appearance: I could plainly distinguish their ferocious countenances; they were as dark in their visages, as, from their appearance, I took them to be in their hearts; they had tremendous mustachios, large brimmed hats and small feathers, cigars in their mouths, pistols in their waist-belts, large mantillas, or cloaks, thrown loosely over them, which nearly covered their horses, and at the bottom of which appeared the end of a huge cutlass. On coming up to me, with a fierce and penetrating look, they sternly said *Bona noche*! This unexpectedly agreeable salutation I politely returned, thinking myself fortunate in passing them so easily; but I suppose, from experience, they had found that there is very little use in robbing a soldier: had I been a merchant, most likely there would have been cause for another monument in this sequestered thicket. I must, however, beg pardon of those gentlemen, if I am wrong in my conjecture; there never being greater room for suspicion, from personal appearances.

At length, I had cleared the wood, and day began to dawn; the sun peeping over the distant hills, and glittering with silvery beauty through the dew-dropping trees. I arrived at a romantic verdant spot, on the banks of a clear brook, when my companion, for indeed a horse, on these occasions, may almost he permitted to claim this appellation, asked permission to stop and take a snack, which he made me understand by stretching his neck out to reach the green herbage under his feet. My feelings being in perfect unison with his, I slipped his bridle off and turned him out to graze, and seating myself on a craggy projecting bank by the stream, ate what the contents of my haversack afforded, which I qualified with draughts of the clear water at my feet,

I now perceived a great dust at a distance, and I could not surmise what else was advancing to arrest my farther progress, on this tedious little journey; indeed, I now fancied myself another knight errant, which I certainly was, as far as regarded my Rosinante, for it was the counterpart of that celebrated animal.

The dust, accompanied with great noise and glitter of arms, was fast approaching, and my mind was soon - relieved from conjecture, by seeing the 27th British regiment coming up to join the army. I now mounted my horse, and continued my journey. Here I could not help observing the long rear this regiment had, while our battalion, from being hardened to the climate, and used to the roads, kept together like a swarm of bees, exhibiting the striking contrast between a regiment that had become veterans in the country, and those who had just landed.

The reason was obvious; the feet of the latter not being hardened to the soil, were easily blistered, which caused the number of stragglers I met. I am convinced this gallant regiment will not be hurt at my remark, as I apprehend all are much in the same way on their first arrival.

Soon after passing this regiment, I reached Aldeigolega, the place of my destination, and glad enough I was to get into a billet. I got some tea, and my horse some straw, which is here almost their only food, and then went to bed; the only one in which I had slept for the last nine months. I thought with pleasure of my safe arrival, with so few obstructions, on so lonely and dismal a road; and soon resigned myself to a sleep so sound, that I did not even dream of ghosts, wild beasts, or *banditti*.

CHAPTER 7

# Gibraltar

*Here Britain's matchless fortress frown'd from high,*
*Proud on the lofty and stupendous rock,*
*Where awful nature spurns the aid of art*
*To guard her giant strength; defiance hold,*
*The island mistress of the mighty seas*
*Hurl'd from its summit, to the vain attempt*
*Of foes to dispossess her of her reign*
*Over the narrow water, that divides*
*Europe's fair realms from Afric's burning shore.*

Clark's *Siege*

Haying arrived at Lisbon, we remained there a few days, and were then ordered to embark for England. We got rid of all our camp-equipage and cattle, which compelled me very reluctantly to dispose of my old friend, Fawn (this name I had given my horse, on account of its colour); but I took care to procure him a good master, for no servant better deserved one.

In our passage we were much buffeted about by bad weather, and driven into the Scilly islands: here we remained some time wind-bound, which did not much displease us; for they are most delightfully situated, living is remarkably cheap, and the inhabitants gave us an idea of old England again. From the many hardships we had experienced in the country we had just left, we fancied this plentiful place a complete retreat of security and contentment; and had I had my choice, I would gladly have accepted a snug little cot, with competency and tranquillity, in these sweet little islands, in preference to an unsettled dukedom of the continent; and would willingly have resigned the delicious wines, choice fruits, and tempting viands, of the Peninsula, with all its broils and contentions, for this peaceful abode.

Quitting this rocky harbour, we arrived at Gosport, where we landed, as may easily be conceived, in a most motley and tattered condition. Our coats were patched over with different coloured cloth, for which purpose we had even cut off our skirts. My own coat was mended with the breeches of a dead Frenchman, which I found on the field—the only trophy I yet had to boast of having retained from the spoils of the enemy. In this state we marched for Salisbury, when we were invited to dine with the Mayor and Corporation of that town. It so happened that.I sate next to a major of the local militia, whose splendid uniform and sparkling epaulettes, contrasted with my thread-worn patched jacket and mud-like looking shoulder-knot, once so brilliant on these parades, afforded a fertile source of amusement for the jocose part of the company. However, the jest was rather in my favour,—a circumstance which caused some mortification to my bedizened neighbour.

In this town our battalion was broken up; each detachment proceeding to join its respective regiment. I marched with mine to Lewes, in Sussex; and on our arrival we certainly cut a very ludicrous appearance, from our ragged state, but were received with a hearty welcome by our long-lost comrades, after so long an absence. We were now, however, able to get at our heavy baggage, and undergo a thorough refit, so that I again appeared bedecked in new finery, and, forgetting all my past troubles, I strutted, and dressed, and thought myself as fine a fellow as ever; but these splendid trappings, alas! were also doomed ere long to be dyed of a deeper stain than those they had replaced.

We had only remained in our native land about six weeks, when we were again ordered on foreign service. We left Lewes barracks, and marched for Portsmouth, where we embarked for Gibraltar, at which fortress we arrived after a tedious passage of five weeks.

Having landed here, we commenced garrison-duty, which was much more severe than we expected to find it, for we frequently had not more than one night in bed, and the next on guard. This was extremely unpleasant, for though we had now got rid of our former companions—the scorpions and centipedes, yet these were superseded by wooden beds in general swarming with bugs; and the rooms were besides so infested with rats, that we were obliged to collect all the bones and scraps that remained at dinner, and, on lying down on the stretcher at night, leave them on the floor for these gentry to devour, in order to prevent their scampering over our faces as we lay asleep, and gnawing the powder and *pomatum* out of our hair; indeed, had we slept too soundly between, the reliefs, they would probably have commenced on the *pericranium* itself. All this, however, was ease and luxury in comparison to campaigning, for here we had a warm room, good food, and a comfortable barrack to retreat to, after being relieved. Indeed, on the whole, the Rock is rather a desirable quarter for soldiers, particularly the private men, as it is impossible they can live better in any part of the world. They have a good basin of coffee or cocoa for breakfast, good meat, soup, and vegetables, for dinner, and bread and cheese for supper; wine and spirits being so cheap that they commonly get too much of them.

Here our time passed on very agreeably; sometimes we dined with the governor, and other families in the garrison, or went to balls, concerts, and evening parties. Before dinner, we generally promenaded on the saluting battery, or retired from the heat to the more edifying lounge of a grand library: occasionally we explored the Rock, rode on the neutral ground, or bathed.

This place has, however, great disadvantages, particularly its being so subject to autumnal pestilential fevers,—a calamity very fatal in this climate: they break out with the most direful effects, and in their malignancy may almost vie with the plague. During this season the garrison is exceedingly unpleasant, owing to the sultry and languid heat, which is almost insupportable when coming from the Levant, or eastward: at this time every duty is extremely oppressive, from the relaxed and low state of the system caused by this unwholesome and contagious air. I have been on the barrier-guard and frequently opened the gates during the night, to let cart-loads of the dead bodies of those to whom this disease had proved fatal pass through to the neutral ground for interment. A Lazaretto was, however, soon established, and its construction was attended with the most beneficial consequences.

At this season the communication with Spain is constantly closed, which renders the necessaries of life very dear; I have known ten dollars given for a turkey, three shillings for a pound of butter, and sixpence for an egg, &c.

An expedition had been fitted out at this port, under the command of Lieutenant-general Lord Blaney, for the purpose, as we understood, of making a descent on Malaga, in which my regiment received orders to embark. Being shipped on board an old Spanish man-of-war, under jury-masts, we proceeded after the expedition with all sail possible, but only reached them as this unfortunate affair was terminating, and that with the greatest disaster. Our flank companies, however, landed to support them; but support was now almost too late, for they were withdrawing in the greatest confusion and haste to our boats, into which they got, and which ought to have been sent back for the remainder of the regiment. The artillery was lost, and a great number of prisoners taken, among whom was the Commander-in-chief himself; but the greater part of the troops had the good fortune to escape under the fire of the *Rodney* man-of-war, and our flank companies, who were the last that re-embarked.

We left this old hulk and went into transports, where we were a little more comfortable, not having taken off our clothes from the time we left the Rock till now—about a fortnight; lying all this time about fifty of us together on the cabin floor, on a sail-cloth spread out for our accommodation.

We now steered our course for Gibraltar, not too much elated with the laurels we had gained. I will not enter into particulars, as there was no great honour attached to this undertaking; I shall only observe, that those who escaped were exceedingly glad to reach their comfortable station again, after their expedition to Malaga. Indeed we might on the whole consider ourselves very fortunate, as the rotten old Spanish hulk in which we first sailed, soon after went to the bottom, and all hands on board perished; so that the regiment, every man of which was in her but a few days previously, had an almost miraculous escape.

Being again settled in garrison, we remained quietly for some time; but the French soon making their appearance in the neighbourhood, caused us much trouble. They had compelled General Ballasteros with his army to retreat and take refuge under the cover of our guns, together with all the inhabitants of St. Roque, and the villages in its vicinity; which gave the neutral ground the effect of a large country fair, and was at the same time a scene of the greatest distress. The fugitives had fled with their goods, cattle, children, and provisions; but the enemy withdrawing in a short time, these poor people returned to their dwellings, and the duty of the garrison became more easy in consequence. We had thus an opportunity of making excursions to Algeziras, St. Roque, and even to the Castle of Andalusia, which were very pleasant recreations, as a most charming country is to be seen in a few hours' ride.

Having now much leisure, I had an opportunity of seeing all the beauties and curiosities of this strong fortress, for I believe, in point of strength, it has not its equal in Europe; indeed, it appears as if art and nature had combined in rendering it so. Colonel Drinkwater has given so elaborate a description of it in his account of the siege of this place, that it would appear like plagiarism to enlarge on the subject. I may, however, be excused for mentioning some observations I was enabled to make in person on parts of this amazing rock. I visited Saint Michael's cave, which is a most wonderful subterraneous cavern, situated about half-way up to the top of the rock, and nearly in the centre of it; it runs under ground to a distance that has never yet been explored: this wonderful place is rendered extremely Gothic in appearance by its great number of petrified pillars; it is besides very lofty, and when lighted up, which is once a year, it bears a great resemblance to a beautiful cathedral. Its grandeur is greatly enhanced by the glittering lustre of the particles of granite and crystal-like substances, and also by the stately columns formed in rather a pleasingly irregular order, by means of the trickling drops of water, which congeal like icicles, and petrify as they hang from the roof, until they become vast pillars, which seem the support of this monstrous and curious cave.

Leaving this large illuminated cavern, we entered one not so spacious, but more damp and very gloomy: we passed by a pond of clear water; and then, by stooping, got into a passage, which leads downwards, and in which, I was informed, that General O'Hara, when Governor of this fort, went farther than any one has since adventured to proceed, and left his sword as a mark of his progress, and as a reward for those who might be bold enough to go and fetch it; but it still remains, no person having as yet had sufficient resolution.

On our way from this extraordinary place, a circumstance of a trifling nature struck me, which probably would not enter into the elevated minds of those engaged in describing these wonderful fortifications, or the much more wonderful operations of their batteries, when opened on the enemy; their glacis, fascines, scarps and counterscarps, embrasures, *chevaux-de-frise*, ramparts, sallyports, stockades, and *caponnierès*. The exalted ideas of such persons would not descend to notice the trifles that attract the attention of common observers, and by which my mind at this moment was entirely engrossed—I mean the numerous groups of apes and monkeys skipping about the rock; some with their cubs on their backs, others cleaning their little ones and grinning at the dogs that barked at them, setting them at defiance by jumping from rock to rock and throwing stones at them. The circumstance of these animals having taken up their abode on this height can only be accounted for by its producing the *palmato*, *eringo* root, and wild dates, on which it is understood they chiefly subsist: it is, however, very singular, as there are none of them in any other part of Spain, not even on the Malaga mountains, which are contiguous and more fertile; but there are great numbers on the hill opposite, on the Barbary coast, called Ape's Hill; so that it is possible they have a passage from this place under the Straits to Saint Michael's Cave, as its end could never be found, and might have taken the brave exploring General to Africa, had he continued his adventurous exploit. The reader will, I hope, pardon this stretch of conjecture, as I must confess, in this instance, my ideas nearly out-step the bounds of probability. Since writing the above, I am informed that the worthy old General himself was the person who. imported this lively race of bipeds; and, indeed, so partial was he to these queer animals, that, in the goodness of his heart, he even allowed them a regular ration of peas, rice, and other food, till they became familiarized to the spot.

Another expedition, which acted so gallantly at Barossa, being now in this quarter, the flank companies of my regiment were ordered to join it: detachments were also sent to Tariffa and Ceuta; to the last of which places I accompanied them, and we relieved the 4th Regiment, then in possession of the citadel.

We here received every mark of attention and indulgence from the Commandant, General Fraser. Here was no ostentatious parade, no unnecessary duty, so often seen in garrison towns, but a regular good system of subordination and consistency kept up, on which all good and great men pride themselves; and which must give a general satisfaction, not to be expected from that outward, tawdry, and useless show, so often practised. We were entertained by this worthy gentleman with that hospitality and kindness which is peculiar only to well-regulated and domestic families. The Spaniards here were also very polite and attentive, being for the most part *grandee*s who had been obliged to fly, with their families, from their estates, which were confiscated by our common enemy the French, and to take refuge in this place of security. In general, however, they were extremely poor, owing to their loss of property, and their servants were frequently obliged to bring the silver relics of their ancient splendour, and offer them for sale to supply their immediate wants.

We found this a healthy, plentiful and agreeable quarter, in which we partook of every pleasure and amusement; frequenting their *Tertullias, conversationes*, bullfights, &c. We were also highly entertained by their *fandangos, boleros*, concertos, and *serenatas*; but what struck me the most, on meeting the ladies the day after these parties, was to observe their condescension and affability in addressing their partners in the dance; a custom so much neglected with us; or if by chance observed, amounting only to a slight inclination of the head, hardly perceptible.

This extensive fortress was almost the reverse of that I had just left: the one had been rendered the strongest of fortifications by nature; the other by art. It contains tiers upon tiers of ramparts, with a great many drawbridges, &c. Instead of passing only one, as at Gibraltar, we here went over at least half-a-dozen, on the way to the neutral ground, with an equal number of covert-ways, strongly barricaded; and, to add to its wonderful security, it has been made an artificial island. Indeed, these two projecting rocks may well be called the pillars of Hercules; for two such are scarcely again to be met with, possessing such astonishing strength.

After having passed the different barriers above-mentioned, we arrived on a fine open plain, with a hill on the left which commands the garrison. From this side, on turning to take a view of the fort, I could not but admire its prodigious strength; having been once employed on an expedition to take it; and surmised there would have been many a broken head on the occasion, had the project been executed.

This plain is neutral between the Moors and Spaniards; on passing it, you are in the territories of the Emperor of Morocco. Sentries from the Barbary troops are placed on these borders, whom you must pass on entering their country. Having an inclination to do this, in company with a gentleman in the Commissariat, I approached them, and a most singular race of beings they were. They sat at the door of a little hut (which was their guardhouse) on the grass, with their legs across, like so many tailors at work, with beards hanging down to their waist, high turbans on their heads, and in their mouths long pipes, which reached about two yards from them and rested on the ground. Their complexions are exceedingly swarthy, and they have a dirty and shabby appearance.

On coming up to their post, I made them understand by signs that I wanted to pass, which they agreed to, but would not acquiesce in the request of the Commissary to accompany me, taking him from his blue uniform to be a Spaniard, to which nation they have a mortal hatred; they, therefore, in a careless morose manner, permitted me to go alone. I went with an intention of visiting a large *seraglio*, which is seen at a distance: but when I got about half-way I began to consider the danger of trusting myself among these barbarians, and, as second thoughts are sometimes best, I resolved to turn back; for, had these Mahometans taken me into the interior of their country and condemned me to perpetual slavery, who would have been able to have obtained my ransom, or where could I have applied for redress? These apprehensions induced me to hasten back to the garrison, quite satisfied with my travels in Africa.

In this delightful and healthy situation we had remained about six weeks, when, being relieved by part of the 26th Regiment, we again embarked to join our battalion, and enter anew upon actual service.

On our arrival at the Rock, we found the regiment all bustle going on board, in consequence of orders to join again the grand army in Portugal We soon reached Lisbon, and landed there; when we found that the lines of circumvallation were broken up, the French having retreated; and that the forces under Marshal Marmont and the Duke of Wellington were some hundreds of miles up the country, manoeuvring in sight of each other: we, therefore, lost no time in equipping for the field.

## Chapter 8
# The Horrors of Retreat

*Here what thousands fell in vain,*
*Wasted with disease and anguish—*
*Not in glorious battle slain.*

Hosier's *Ghost*

Being soon furnished with tents, for we now received these necessary encumbrances, which on our former services in this country had not been the case, and having provided ourselves with baggage animals and all other field-equipage, we set out to undertake a campaign, perhaps one of the most arduous ever encountered by British troops.

The drum now summoned us from the capital of Portugal; we ascended the Tagus some distance in boats, and landed at Villa Franca, whence we proceeded, by forced marches, to overtake our army, previous to its being engaged. Expresses continually met us on the road to hasten our movement, as an action was every moment expected to take place; and we had barely time to give nature sufficient repose, as we continued marching nearly night and day towards Salamanca. We found this excessively harassing, as the weather was in its height of summer heat. We at length reached Ciudad Rodrigo, where we were obliged to halt one day, leaving two officers and some men sick from fever brought on by extreme exertion. Having nearly reached Salamanca, we heard the sound of cannon-shot all through the day; and on arriving at that town we learned that an action had taken place, which rendered all our forced marches useless. The enemy were, as usual after a battle, flying; and we still continued, if not increased, our exertions to come up with the army, which was now on the high-road to Madrid, leaving behind us at this place more officers and men that had fallen sick. We passed over the distressing yet glorious field of Salamanca, about the third day after the battle,—a scene, if possible, more horrid to us than if we had been in the battle itself and gone on with the conquering army. The ground was now become disgusting from the number of dead that lined the roads; and these, from their putrescent state, caused by the heat, were so obnoxious, that we were obliged to stop our noses with our pocket-handkerchiefs as we went along, to prevent contagion; which, in spite of all precaution, proved as fatal to us, as if we had actually been in the action.

I left my comrade sick on the road; and on the next day's march I was taken so ill myself, that I was obliged to go back and join him. Our sickness proved to be a fever of the most malignant kind, and we were in consequence obliged to return to the sick depot at Salamanca. Although I had a horse, I was so extremely ill that I could not sit on it, and we were occasionally laid together on a bullock-car, to be conveyed to the city. In our way we had to re-pass this dreadful scene of decayed bodies,—a circumstance which appeared to add to our disease, which was also increased by a rough road of many leagues, on a still more rough and disagreeable carriage. The jolting of the conveyance, the intense heat of the sun, and the raging state of my blood caused by the burning fever, made me try to get out of this uncouth carriage, wishing to lay myself down by the road-side, and there take my chance, in preference to being so tormented by this painful method of conveyance; for the bullocks, being bit by the flies, would run and plunge over rugged stones out of the common track; indeed, death itself would have been preferable to a long continuance of this wretched existence: although burning with thirst, we had not water to moisten our parched tongues; and, to add to our misery, my poor fellow-sufferer would exclaim that he was dying, and that I was not half so bad as he was, and I, on the other hand, did not pity him, conceiving I was in a much more deplorable situation. In this state of wretchedness we arrived at the wished-for town, and billets were procured for us; but on being conducted to mine, the inhabitants were gone out. This circumstance obliged me to lie on the steps of the door till they returned, which was in a few hours. On the arrival of the hostess, who was an old widow-woman, she had me directly taken in, and a bed prepared for me, as well as she, being very poor, was able. The bed was on the floor in one corner of the room; however, it was such as generally fell to our subordinate lot. Having, with the assistance of this good woman, got into bed, my servant went in search of a doctor, but he could not procure one at that late hour. Here I lay in a most miserable condition, till my man, Standfast, came in the morning to know what I would take for breakfast, "Take! my good fellow," said I; "what can be got?" He replied that there was a little tea left, after dividing our small stock with my brother Sub on parting.

"But then, Sir," added he, "there is no sugar, milk, bread, butter, or any thing besides."

Here was a state for a sick man to be in! not a farthing of money had I seen since I left Lisbon; therefore, I desired him to take one of my shirts, and with what sum he could get for it, to buy some sugar, milk, butter, and bread; he went, and soon brought me these necessary articles. The money for which he had disposed of the shirt was a *pistreen* and a half—about half-a-crown; nearly six months before I had given a guinea for it: but what I now got in exchange was of much more value to me.

This day a doctor came to me: he told me I was very ill, and sent me some medicine, and desired I would get some chocolate, some lemons to make lemonade, and other necessaries; I therefore told my trusty servant, Thomas, to take another shirt, which reduced my stock to two; and with this supply he procured me what was requisite. He also brought me an account of one of our officers lying dead in the town, and that my poor comrade was not likely to live the night out. This news affected me very much; but from my weak state of health and depressed condition of mind, I resigned myself to the thoughts of soon experiencing their fate.

On the following morning, finding that my little stock of comforts was gone, I sent Thomas with another of the aforesaid linen articles to procure more, which reduced me to my last shirt; indeed, I might say, my last shift. However, he got what he could purchase with so small a sum, and brought me intelligence of the fate of my poor companion, who had now ended all his miseries, toils, and troubles. Standfast likewise mentioned that he had met a surgeon of my acquaintance, whom he had seen visiting me at Gibraltar, and who was now on duty at this depot I immediately sent him in search of this gentlemen, whom he had the good fortune to find; and in whom he brought me not only a doctor, but a friend and a benefactor. This worthy man, whom gratitude bids me mention, is now surgeon of the 85th Regiment of foot: on seeing me, he could not help shaking his head, then taking me by the hand, he said, "You are certainly very ill; but keep up your spirits, and I will send you some medicine that will do you good; then buy a fowl, and get some broth made, and barley-water, and some——" He was going on, when I interrupted him, by asking him how I was to procure these necessaries?—"Why, buy them, to be sure!"

This was a sore reply, which he soon perceived; and guessing by my dejected countenance the state of my purse, he immediately asked if I had not money for that purpose: I frankly, but with a heavy heart, told him I had not. He made no reply; wishing, I suppose, not to add to the distress of my feelings, already too much overpowered: but taking me kindly again by the hand, and giving me a friendly squeeze, left me; and returning in a short time, put half a doubloon by my bed-side, at the same time desiring I would let him know when I wanted more; telling me that, as the fever had now abated, I stood less in need of medicine than real comforts; and that had those officers of my regiment just deceased had them, they might still have been alive.

A few days after, when the fever had quite left me, he sent me from the hospital, wine, baked rice-puddings, tea, &c., and with the money I got one of my shirts back, the rest having been disposed of; I also bought grapes, melons, chocolate, and all kinds of necessaries; being now pronounced in a state of convalescence. My old landlady, during the whole time, gave me all the assistance and attention that her age and poverty would permit.

I now began to walk about and take the air, gaining strength very fast, and went to pay a visit to my friend the doctor, who informed me that I had been dangerously ill; that my tongue was black with disease, and that he had even doubted of my recovery, on which he now congratulated me.

On my way to his billet, my old hostess, who accompanied me part of the way, pointed out a poor, mean, antique-looking house, and informed me it had been in olden time an apothecary's shop, which had been kept by a Doctor San Grado, a man who had been famous in his day for the simpleness and efficacy of his remedies; in short, she told me it was the identical house in which dwelt that prince of the Esculapian school, from whom Le Sage took the great character he so humorously and admirably delineated. Notwithstanding the encomiums of this good lady, I certainly found an inward pleasure that I had not been placed, during my late illness in his hands, as I fancied his copious draughts of warm water and incessant bleeding would not have recovered me so soon as my kind doctor's more experienced practice, and modern mode of treatment.

Being in this improving state of health, and walking, one day with a friend for the purpose of recruiting my. strength, we perceived a bullock-car coming in, and, to my surprise, two more officers of my regiment on it, in a most miserable condition. We went and procured them billets; and having got the worse-looking object of the two into one, we took the other poor fellow into his: he begged for a mattress to be spread on the floor, to lie upon, while the bed was preparing, being so exhausted that he could not stand. This being complied with, he stretched himself on it, and in a few minutes paid his debt of nature. A finer young man was rarely to be seen; his countenance even after death displayed more colour and animation than that of many persons when alive. This poor. fellow had also been destitute of money, and consequently of every kind of comfort to be procured by its all-powerful aid. However, "out of evil cometh good;" for these unfortunate deaths, caused in a great measure by privations, reaching, head-quarters, our. good Commander-in-chief directly issued orders that all sick officers in future should be supplied with necessary comforts from the hospitals, in the- same manner as the men, which ever afterwards was the case; which kind act of humanity, I am convinced, will be remembered with lasting gratitude by those gentlemen who have benefited by it.

After being here about six weeks, I found myself perfectly recovered, and was ordered to march a strong detachment, composed of different regiments, to Madrid: this duty I performed accordingly, and arrived there before my regiment, who were halted at Cuellar; but I am afraid the reader will find it too tedious to follow my irksome steps through this heavy march; I shall therefore merely say, that I reached the Spanish capital, with my men, in good health and spirits.

Madrid is certainly a very fine city; but does not answer the description the Spaniards give of it, who call it "the metropolis of the world." The principal streets are spacious, and the buildings very fine, particularly the Palace, which is much enriched by the great improvements at that time making by their French King Joseph. What, however, struck me most forcibly, were the grand streets, terminating in as grand and spacious avenues, shaded in the most agreeable manner by stately and wide-spreading trees. In these walks are numberless delightful fountains of the most cool and refreshing nature, around which, sitting and walking, may be seen the most elegant, and though not fair, yet most charming of the fair; but these great inducements for taking the air, were, however, in a great measure suppressed, by the unusual number of miserable objects of charity, every moment begging alms in the most suppliant manner,—an appearance which greatly diminished the attraction of these recreative groves.

Indeed, I never witnessed greater scenes of human misery than this town presented. This state of things naturally resulted from the heavy contributions, and other arbitrary sufferings, which the inhabitants had endured while groaning under the yoke of their late intruders. As a proof of this, I was informed that there were generally every morning several of these poor wretches found dead in the streets, who had perished in the night with cold and hunger, the concomitant evils of those countries which, from the ambition or policy of their rulers, are made the theatre of war. God forbid that my own dear land should ever experimentally feel that dreadful scourge!

Here I visited all the public places, particularly the Museum, which far exceeds my powers of description. It consisted of the rarest curiosities; the finest paintings, by Rubens, Raphael, Michael Angelo, &c.; an excellent assortment of fossils, minerals, and shells, birds, beasts, and fishes; besides a most magnificent display of diamonds, jewels, massy pieces of gold, and all kinds of precious stones, the produce of the Peruvian mines, so renowned for their inexhaustible store of wealth. It was to me a subject of infinite surprise that the French should not have laid their plundering hands upon these immense treasures. On farther consideration, however, I supposed the reason to be, that their King knew very well we should not disturb them, and that there was every probability of his returning to take possession of them; which, indeed, was very soon the case.

We visited the palace, which is really superb, particularly with regard to the tapestry, pictures, furniture, and the great number of clocks and watches, one of which is in every chamber. In one of these apartments, I observed, in the middle of a beautiful mahogany table, a most brilliant and valuable diamond, set in gold, which had been spoiled by a French soldier getting in, and with his bayonet trying to dig it out; but being caught in the fact, he was obliged to desist, having left ocular demonstration of his roguish intention.

This, certainly, is a most stately palace, and when finished, will no doubt be one of the finest in Europe; being situated on an eminence, commanding a most extensive and charming prospect, having in its front a river and gardens, which in point of beauty and magnificence will correspond with this pompous edifice.

As to their operas, theatres, and public places of amusement, I saw none of them, either here, or in any other place that I have been (I do not even except Paris), that could at all be compared to our own; and any regular description of their public buildings, fountains, bridges, churches, &c., or of their carnivals, tournaments, and bull-fights, on my part, even were I competent to the task, would be an intrusion, after their having been frequently and minutely depicted by many able travellers, and would besides be too great a digression from a confined narrative.

From this great city I proceeded to join my regiment, then quartered in the Escurial, certainly an uncommon place, rendered famous, not for its beautiful palace, but for its enormous pile of buildings. It is situated in a sequestered spot, at the foot of the Guarderama mountains, and is built, they say, in the form of a gridiron; but for my part, I could not see that it had any shape at all, except the most confused. It was erected by Philip the Second of Spain,, in commemoration of a vow he had made for a victory gained over the Moors, on the day of St. Lawrence, to whom this structure is dedicated, and who is said to have suffered martyrdom on the utensil that this building is supposed to represent, and from which it takes its name.

This palace was now converted into our barracks; indeed, I believe there is room enough to accommodate twenty thousand men here, so large is this astonishing fabric.

Here we remained but a short time, when the regiment received the route for Pinto, a large village some miles beyond the capital. I was detained a few days, and then proceeded after them; and during the long day's march, which was about seven leagues, was overtaken by a most violent thunder-storm, that greatly delayed my journey, and made it very late at night when I arrived again at Madrid. Every house was shut, and there was no possibility of obtaining a billet. After wandering about the streets for some time, I luckily found out my old quarter, I knocked at the door, and it was speedily opened. The people did not recollect me at first, from the wet and dirty plight I was in; but they soon welcomed me in, made a fire to dry me, got me some supper, and prepared my bed. I have often heard this generous nation railed against, and have even done it myself; but when we reflect we were among a persecuted people, whose language we were not masters of, whose manners and customs are so different from our own, and whose religion we so much ridicule and despise; when we consider that we were imposed upon their families as inmates, and remember how often that privilege was abused, and recollect that they still continued to invite us to their daily fare,—when I think of this generosity, and know how often they were, in return for it, disregarded, contemptuously treated, offended by us, and sometimes robbed by our servants, I cannot but wonder they had the patience to treat us so kindly as they did. With regard to their troops, whom we so much scorn, I have no hesitation in saying that they possess physical properties which would render them equal to any in the world, had they the advantages we enjoy, of being well-officered, well disciplined, and serving under a wise and judicious Government. They would then, indeed, be a great military nation, and sufficiently able to fight their own battles; but of all these advantages they are unfortunately destitute.

Having again quitted Madrid, I came up with my regiment at Pinto, in the beautiful province of La Mancha, famous for the birth-place of the renowned knight of the rueful countenance, and celebrated for its delicious wines: I took this opportunity of seeing their vaults, which, from their amazing extent, were well worth notice. Here were exceeding large vases in which the wine stood the year round, without any covering except what was formed by the lees, a thick scum something like yeast, caused by the fermentation. This being well incrusted together, answered much better than a wooden covering; for as the wine is drawn off it gradually sinks with it, and thereby keeps the air out and the wine sound, although it is constantly on the draught. These large vessels put me in mind of the story of the forty thieves getting into the different barrels: had they been here, I think they might have all got into one of these pretty little tubs, and there remained quite at their ease.

Another great advantage to us was the luxuriant abundance of fruit that every where presented itself. It being now their vintage, their houses were stored with it: the chamber which I occupied was decorated in a very tasteful manner, the ceiling being hung with festoons of the most beautiful clusters of grapes, and delicious verdant melons, here and there garnished with the finest figs and other fruits, in order to preserve them for winter use.

This place was also noted for its amazingly large pigeon-houses; they were of equal extent, and at a distance had an appearance resembling that of gentlemen's seats in my country. They were adapted entirely to the breed of these birds, for the supply of the Madrid and other markets, as they are a very common article of food in this kingdom.

Although still destitute of money, yet in this abundant country we managed to procure many comforts besides our rations. As for the fruit, the inhabitants had no objection to our eating what we chose, frequently giving us wine and other presents: but as it often happened that where we found ourselves the most comfortable we remained the shortest time, so it proved here; for we had to continue our advance till we came to the pretty village of Ciempucellas, situated on a river, on the opposite side of which was the fine town of Aranjues, where the enemy were in great force.

Here we left our cantonments, and again took the field. I was sent with a party of men to the river that divided us, to throw up breast-works at the bridge, in order to obstruct the enemy should they attempt to cross; but, after being at work the whole day, I had the mortification of seeing all our labour blown into the air, according to orders received for that purpose, the more effectually to prevent their crossing.

News now arrived of the siege of Burgos being raised, and the army under the Duke of Wellington on its retreat. In consequence of this information, General Lord Hill also commenced a retreat, in order to form a junction with the Burgos army. The night that preceded this movement I was on piquet, with about seventy men, having strict orders to guard a ford by which the enemy's cavalry were expected every moment to cross, and to make every resistance in my power, but on no account to give way; and that, as soon as they heard me engaged, I should receive support. This of course kept me on the alert the whole night, expecting every moment to see their dragoons plunge into the river to ford it, as they were in great numbers on the other side, and ready accoutred: fortunately for me they did not attempt it, although they kept up a great noise and bustle the whole night, which was merely a *ruse de guerre*, as they crossed a few miles higher up.

At day break we were called in, and I had to join my regiment; to gain which, after being on the advance about four miles, I had to ascend an exceedingly high hill, almost a day's march in itself: and I had hardly time to take a little refreshment when we were ordered to fall in.

A retreat now commenced, such as perhaps surpassed any that British troops had hitherto encountered: the Corunna retreat, from what I experienced of it, and the opinion that I have heard, given by those officers who were on both, will bear no comparison with this.

We moved off our ground about mid-day; and about five in the evening it began to rain, which seemed to increase as we moved through the dark and dismal night. As the day began to dawn, the weather became clearer; and we now made greater progress, halting only a few minutes at a time, when necessity compelled us; and late in the evening lay down on some ploughed land by the road-side, after a march of about ten leagues across a fine country; but the finest country is, from the depth of soil, in general, the most difficult to get over in bad weather. Such was the case here: on this swampy bed, after eating a melon, the only thing I had left, I was so overcome with fatigue and hard marching, that I fell fast asleep; and, in all probability I should have remained there till this time, had I not been roused by the men. As we proceeded, the sun, now darting his fiercest rays upon our dewy garments, made them smoke as if we had been drying our wet and miry clothes by a good fire.

It was deplorable here to behold the beautiful villages, in which we had so lately and pleasantly been quartered, left to the mercy of those who were about to take possession of them. The inhabitants had fled; their fine fruit had been taken by the troops; and it was with the greatest difficulty, and even severity, that we could restrain them from taking too much of the strong wine, which was now let flow into the vaults, to prevent it from falling into the hands of the French.

At last we reached the stately avenues leading to the capital, which now looked gloomy enough, where we halted, and the troops got as much biscuit as they could carry, with other provisions, and an allowance of rum. The rest of the stores were destroyed; and the remaining casks of wine and spirits stove in, and let run into the street in the greatest profusion, to prevent its becoming a booty to the enemy; who were now close at our heels. We remained here barely sufficient time to receive our rations, and then continued our retrograde movements. The next day we came into the vicinity of the Guadarama mountains, where, from the increased fatigue, excessive marching, and exposure to the nightly damps of the field, I was seized with a swelling in my legs, that obliged me to go on in front, being in consequence placed on my horse: I was unwilling to mount him before from the poor state he was in for want of food, but necessity now compelled me to ride him. I went on, through that day and the following night, endeavouring to re-cross these prodigious mountains: when I had nearly attained their summit, I saw on the road what I conceived to be a flock of wild turkeys; but, on a near approach, I discovered them to be a flight of large vultures, or eagles, voraciously devouring a horse that had died on the way. These birds paid very little regard to me on my passing them: they merely flew up, and hovered over my head; and no sooner had I passed, than they pounced down on their carrion, and continued their feast. I must confess I did not at all like the look of these monstrous birds, being somewhat afraid of their attacking my poor steed, which was in very little better plight than the one on which they were so ravenously feeding.

I proceeded in the greatest torture till I descended these mountains; when I found myself in such a state from rheumatism, that I was obliged to be taken off the horse, and carried into a cow-house near the road. Here I lay in great agony: but, by a fortunate circumstance, the surgeon of the regiment coming to this place with some sick men, bathed my feet in spirits, which gave me great relief, and the next morning I found myself much better; but still I could neither walk, nor ride on horseback, from the pain I suffered: I was, therefore, put into a spring-wagon, in which I rode the greatest part of the day. I may here allowably advert to the usefulness of this Royal Corps.: for, although they did not go into extreme danger themselves, they were the means of taking others both into it, and out of it.

On arriving at a cross-road, where the army turned off and proceeded by a different route, I was taken out of the wagon, and again placed on my horse, which my servant had with him, and was desired to proceed to Arviola, where I was informed there was a depot: but, on arriving at that place, I did not meet with a single British soldier in the town; and so far from its being a depot, it was entirely deserted, with the exception of a Spanish regiment of dragoons, fully accoutred and in readiness to abandon it to the enemy, who were now very near. In this state of affairs, necessity compelled me to go to the Alcalde for billets. He told me that he was much astonished at our application (for I had, on entering this town, overtaken an officer who was very ill, and who had also been misinformed); that the French were seen very distinctly from his balcony, advancing on this place; that they had set the fine town of Segovia on fire, and that the smoke was also visible from his window. However, strange as it may appear, he gave us billets, and we went in. I do not now recollect of what regiment this poor officer was, nor is it of much importance: he was, like myself, very ill; but necessity compelled us, even in the nice of danger, to seek some refreshment, for nature was now literally sinking under the effects of famine, filth, and disease: therefore, while our servants were feeding the horses, we set about preparing some chocolate, and had just time to drink it, when we were informed that the French were entering the town. We instantly mounted our horses, and joined the cavalcade that were flying on the road, with what valuables they could bring off with them; we were now thrown out of the route of the British army, and pursued by a part of the French; and it was only by the greatest perseverance and diligence that we got out of their reach.

Being now out of the main track, many were the difficulties, in addition to that of preventing ourselves from being taken prisoners, which we had to surmount: but after many days' distressing travelling, and concealing ourselves in the woods by night, existing on what their shades afforded, we reached Salamanca; but in a most filthy and impoverished state, not having taken off our clothes, or changed our linen since the retreat commenced. It is singular that amid all these privations I had completely regained the use of my limbs; and a few days' kind treatment from my good old widow, to whose house I went without ceremony, and who received me in the kindest manner, soon restored me to my former state. I was now, however, able to show her some attention in return; for having a number of soldiers quartered on her, who were, as they often are, extremely inconvenient and troublesome, I got a great part of them removed, and made the rest treat her with proper respect.

In a few days I joined my regiment, previous to which I had the misfortune to see my servant, Thomas Standfast, lodged in the hospital. He in his turn had now become ill: for there were few in these campaigns that had not their portion of illness. I heard soon after I left the town that he had ended his earthly career. Poor fellow! A better soldier, or more honest man did not exist.

The troops had now re-crossed the Tormes, near which the retreating army from Burgos had formed a junction with us:

here we remained in camp several days, when the enemy threatened to cross the river, the bridge of which was, in consequence, blown up; but that did not prevent them from effecting their purpose. They forded it in spite of us, and made their appearance directly in our front; our brigade being in line, with two field-pieces of German artillery in the centre, which were well directed and did much execution, the first shot scattered them in all directions; and they drew off their forces from this quarter, taking with them one of the captains of my regiment prisoner, who was a little in advance on reconnaissance. We remained during the night under arms; and the next day took up another position upon a gravelly soil, where there was not an herb growing, or a stick to light a fire. I remember it was here that I went on duty to demolish some houses of a deserted village, in order to obtain fuel. We remained on this spot during the night; and a door which we brought among other fire-wood served three of us exceedingly well for shelter; as, when evening came on, we wrapped our blankets and cloaks about us, then laying down on the ground, we put the door over us, as it began to rain, which kept us warm and dry till we fell in at daylight. All this time our horses were tied to our arms, there being no other fastening; we afterwards made a fire of the door, and sat round it warming ourselves, and wishing most heartily for something to eat. I had in my haversack some chocolate, about a square each, which was shared among us, and immediately devoured; we choosing to eat it raw, rather than make it into a liquid, as we conceived it to be more substantial diet. One of the three now went to the next division on a venture, and luckily returned with part of a loaf, which in these circumstances completely verified the old adage, "That half a loaf is better than no bread." He generously shared it amongst us; and I certainly round it one of the most delicious morsels I had ever eaten. This brave man, I am sorry to say, had the misfortune to have that very arm, which he so benevolently stretched out to relieve us, shot off in the next action in which we were engaged.

The whole army being now collected, took up a new and

more advantageous position on the Aripales, a name then rendered famous by the late most glorious victory; it being the very ground on which the battle of Salamanca was fought. The relics of bones and other fragments that still strewed these memorable hills, struck such terror into the French army, by reminding them of a spot so fatal to them, that they dared not attack us in this position, but endeavoured to outflank us; which our chief observing, ordered his troops to continue the most rapid and retrograde movement, in order to prevent this numerous army, which, according to report, was about one hundred thousand men, cavalry and infantry, from getting into our rear; as our own forces consisted of only about thirty thousand English, and fifteen thousand Portuguese: but of the force of our allies, the Spaniards, I could form no idea, and indeed it was of little consequence.

At the time of our receiving orders to recede from this place, we were dividing the only provisions that had been served out to us for the last two days, which were some starved bullocks; but, from the hurry of the moment, we were obliged to leave the greater part behind us. I saw those men who were fortunate enough to get some, tearing the raw flesh from the bones on the march, like so many hungry hounds gnawing carrion.

The mention of hounds reminds me of a singular statement I met with in *The Journal of a Soldier*—he says:

> I at this time got a post, being for fatigue, with other four. We were sent to break biscuit, and make a mess for Lord Wellington's hounds. I was very hungry, and thought it a good job at the time, as we got our fill while we broke the biscuit—a thing I had not got for some days. When thus engaged, the prodigal son never once was out of my mind; and I sighed, as I fed the dogs, over my humble situation and ruined hopes.

In justice to the great Commander, to whom we are so much indebted for the judicious arrangement of his commissariat, and the anxiety manifested by him upon all occasions to administer to our wants in the field, and our comforts when sick, I cannot omit making some observations on this report. That such a circumstance might have happened in one solitary instance, I admit—I am not impeaching the man's veracity; but that it was of frequent or general occurrence I utterly deny. Upon many occasions, even the most anxious endeavours of the Duke for the welfare of his troops failed, from the impracticability of procuring supplies; and that this was the case at this critical juncture I well know, as I was also with my regiment and in the rear-division of the army at that unhappy period.—The scarcity of bread and biscuit was certainly very great, as I have already mentioned,—so much so that I should imagine it was almost impossible to have procured it for the hounds of the Duke, had he been disposed to have them so fed: but, in the first place, it should be remembered, that there were always servants in charge of these dogs, for the purpose of feeding and taking care of them; and at this moment we could not move one hundred yards without coming in contact with either a dead horse, ox, mule, or ass, which, if I know any thing of hounds, they would much rather make a meal of, than bruised biscuit; indeed, they must have been so fall of carrion at this time, that I have my doubts whether they would have eaten such a mess at all. But, supposing they would have tasted it, where could it have been procured, unless there might have been some saved by the hounds' attendants from the stores at Alba de Tormes, which otherwise would have been destroyed (there being no mode of conveying it away to prevent it falling into the hands of the enemy), after our men had been supplied with as much as they could conveniently carry. The relater of this anecdote may not have been intentionally malicious, but, from the manner in which it is told, the reader would be led to infer, that if he attended on the dogs one day, it would be the turn of some one else another; in feet, that it was a regular duty. Such a conclusion would imply that the hounds "fared sumptuously every day," while the soldiers were not even so well off as the dogs at the rich man's table—not being allowed to feed upon their crumbs. Another circumstance which strikes me most forcibly is, that these animals are reckoned among the baggage of an army: then what brings this species of baggage in the rear, when every other is in front, on a retreat? If they had been blood-hounds, it is most probable this would have been their station; but, as harmless harriers, I cannot conceive why they should have been allowed to remain there.

It is considered no bad food to give dogs, when carrion is not to be had, the sweepings of the commissariat biscuit stores, when conveniently obtained; but at this time I cannot conceive how men could take such pains about dogs, when flesh was so plentiful. Indeed, had biscuit been given to the hounds daily at this serious moment, such conduct would have been sufficient to have caused a mutiny in an army labouring, as it then was, under privations of so severe a nature.

This occurrence may, as I have already said, be true, and mentioned without any malignant design; but I cannot refrain from remarking that there appears to me, in the manner of making the statement, a desire of impressing on the public mind an idea that Lord Wellington took more interest in the fate of his hounds than in that of his troops,—a supposition too revolting to be for a moment entertained. That Lord Byron, who has so egregiously misrepresented the affair, should have been among the number misled by this statement, I am much surprised. A man of his transcendent talents might have known, that the mind of a Commander-in-chief of such an army, under such circumstances, must have matter of much more consequence to occupy his attention than that of feeding of hounds! I am aware that this aspersion is not of sufficient magnitude to attract the notice of the illustrious Chief; but I feel it incumbent on me, as a British officer, to make my observations on what appears to me an attempt to affix so unmerited a slur on the character of that great man.

But to return from this digression, for which I am persuaded no apology will be considered necessary, to the thread of my narrative; I have mentioned the circumstance of the men being compelled to feed upon the raw flesh they could procure; and, indeed, had we halted, cooking was out of the question: it would have given the men more fatigue in dressing their meat, than the nutriment of it would have afforded them strength; the wood being far too wet for the purpose of lighting fires. The rainy season had now completely set in, and our retreat, at this time, was almost as incessant as the rain. The difficulties, privations, and hardships we encountered, were probably almost as severe as those endured in the retreat of the French from Moscow, with the exception of the distance; and, for myself, I certainly should prefer marching through frost and snow, to rain and mire. I do not think that I exaggerate greatly, in saying that we lost nearly as great a number of men, in proportion, as the ill-fated host of fugitives from Russia.

To increase the misery of our situation, this wet and gloomy weather was rendered still more insufferable by the tempestuous gusts of wind, which now prevailed like the equinoctial gales in this country, but with much greater force; and meeting us in the avenues and defiles through which we passed, drove the rain in our faces with such violence, that many were blown down, and others could scarcely make head against it, and during the short rest we got, in the darkness of the night, we had no other shelter but the thick forest, nor any covering but the cloudy sky, as we frequently did not see our baggage for days together.

This period I consider the worst part of the retreat, and the principal cause of those dire calamities which ensued. We contended with every difficulty, moving slowly through an immense tract of country; for impediments of all kinds prevented our going fast. Our route was on no high road; but through woods, deserts, heaths, mountains, and flats, covered with sheets of water, like the meadows in our own country when overflown by the rivers. How closely the enemy pursued us may easily be conceived, from the dashing General Paget having been overtaken by them in these wilds. The moment we attempted to bivouac, that moment they commenced cannonading us; and under this destructive fire, without covering or food, having every thing to apprehend, have we sat shivering on the cold ground the whole night, praying for daylight to see our way forward. Rising one morning from one of these swampy resting-places, our regiment was ordered to fall in and form square, when the General of Division made his appearance, and severely reprimanded us for the loss of so many men, whom we were obliged to leave on the road to the mercy of the enemy.

In this distressing state we proceeded I may say for about five days together (I speak only of the brigade to which I belonged), without any supply of food from the Commissariat; and the consequences attending this privation will soon be seen. My readers will naturally be surprised at such an assertion, and will inquire how this army could exist. Indeed, their existence can only be attributed to the mercy of an all-bounteous providence; for these very wet and dismal forests, through which we passed, not only afforded us shelter from the cutting winds, but provided a sufficient substitute for bread to save a famishing army. They abounded in acorns of a species quite different from those found in England, growing on a small oak with a prickly leaf, somewhat resembling the holly. These acorns, when boiled or roasted, were as sweet as chestnuts; and even eaten raw, they were very palatable. Besides these, the men sometimes got meat from the bullocks and horses that were dead on the road; the soldiers would run out of the ranks, and with their knives and billhooks cut them up with as much dexterity as butchers in Leadenhall market; then sticking the flesh on their bayonets, they would march on with this chance supply. In this state of suffering and hardship we continued our retreat. The roads (if they deserved that name) were rendered almost impassable: to many indeed, quite so; for several of the poor men at length became so exhausted that they stuck in the mud, and had not strength to extricate themselves; we were therefore obliged to leave them to their fate, for it was now "Every one for himself." Being much worn with dysentery, I went on one day with the baggage-guard, and, with the rest of the troops that passed this route, had to ford upwards of twenty rivers,—a circumstance which every poor fellow on this march will well remember. It was literally nothing less than wading through water, sometimes breast-high, at others knee-deep. I cannot exaggerate the horrors of this retreat, were I even inclined to do so; for many will probably peruse this narrative who had to endure the same conflict with myself.

On this occasion, as I was about to cross the most deep and rapid of these streams, being very weak and tired, I got on my horse, now become as weak as myself, and whose life I only preserved by leading him by my side. However, in order to lessen my difficulty, and imagining that he might be strong enough for this little exertion, I mounted him: but, unfortunately, when about the middle, the poor animal fell down, and plunged me over head and ears into the water; so that, in order to avoid a little wet, I found myself even in no small danger of being drowned, for my foot had got entangled in the stirrup, and I had great trouble in extricating it. On getting out with my horse, I was glad to continue marching, in order to circulate my blood and keep myself from perishing with cold: at last we came to a house, a thing which we had not seen for many days. I went in and got myself warm, roasted some acorns, and prepared some tea, which I had not till now had the means of boiling; this was the last of the little stock I had in my pocket, and proved to me a greater restorative than even Doctor Solomon's Balm of Gilead.

Tea is an article of luxury very little known in this part of the world. Even in the towns, where there is nothing to disturb the business of the shops, it is not to be had at the grocers, as in this kingdom: but should any traveller ask for it as a medicine at an apothecary's, he will be sure to obtain it. I state this circumstance for the information of those who may hereafter travel in any part of the Spanish dominions

As we gradually approached the frontiers of Portugal, we left the forests and flat country behind us, and came into a very mountainous district. We now got occasionally half an allowance of rum, and by chance even a regular supply, till at length we left Ciudad Rodrigo in our rear, beyond which place the French did not pursue us. We then halted a few days, and, for the first time since the retreat had commenced, were quartered in a village: this was called Villa d'Agua, literally, Water-Town,—a name most applicable to the face of the country we had been passing through.

Still we were destitute of money, not having had more than half a month's pay issued out for the last six months; we had, therefore, nothing to exist on but the scanty allowance of the Commissary. After this short respite, we continued retreating, and the weather, as if determined to keep time with us, continued its stormy violence; for it was in the worst part of the year that we were compelled to undertake this severe duty. The latter end of November had arrived when we got into winter-quarters, after continually advancing and retrograding from the time we landed at Lisbon,—a period of about seven months, three of which were spent on this trying retreat. We at last arrived at Momento, a little village at the foot of the Estrella Mountains, and there went into cantonments: and thus ended this disastrous campaign; but the dreadful consequences attending it were only commencing, as will be shown in the sequel of this Narrative.

Chapter 9

# The Battle of Vittoria

*They close in clouds of smoke and dust,*
*With sword-sway and with lances' thrust;*
*And such a yell was there,*
*Of sudden and portentous birth,*
*As if men fought upon the earth,*
*And fiends in upper air:*
*O! life and death were in the shout,*
*Recoil and rally, charge and rout,*
*And triumph and despair.*

*Marmion*

In this little dirty village I got a little dirty billet, such as commonly fell to the lot of officers of my rank, and with which, had it even been worse than it then was, I should have been contented—glad of any shelter from this inclement season. My quarter was in the house of a poor peasant, who gave me a small room, with a straw mattress and a little covering in one corner, and a few stones for a fire-place in another. There was no chimney, the smoke always finding its own passage through the crevices of the tiles. We still remained without any money, which we had almost learnt to do without. Indeed, so much was I in the habit of taking what I could get in the shape of food, that I am ashamed to confess I had nearly robbed this poor family of all their potatoes—such a luxury did I think vegetables with our meagre ration of beef. Had private soldiers been in the house, they probably would not have confined themselves to this article.

An order now arrived for the paymaster to proceed to head-quarters for one month's pay; and he soon returned with the money. This desirable supply gave me the means of purchasing eggs, fruit, flour, &c. from my poor old host, and of otherwise recompensing him for my depredations.

We next moved our quarters to Santa Marhina, which was the nearest village: there not being room enough for us in this, I here got a better billet; indeed, we even began to make ourselves comfortable: the men were in snug quarters, and had good provisions, good fires, warm beds, and fine chocolate for breakfast, with even necessary comfort, and, above all, rest, after their fatigue. But this sudden and welcome change from the greatest sufferings to a state of comfortable repose, was the very cause of our consequent calamities. No sooner were we settled in our cantonments, than we experienced the fatal effects of the almost unparalleled sufferings we had undergone; and the sudden transition, already mentioned, to comparative plenty, brought on the most malignant complaints, especially fever, dysentery, and rheumatism. The entire regiment was on the sick list; for a considerable time we had not a man on parade, not even convalescent men enough to attend the sick: it was therefore found necessary to call in the assistance of the inhabitants; indeed, we were now in such a deplorable state, that a staff-surgeon and four assistants were sent us, in addition to our own,—so much did we stand in need of medical aid. With respect to hospitals, nearly half the houses in the village were converted to that purpose. It was truly distressing to see the situation of this fine regiment, which had only landed about seven months previously upwards of a thousand strong, and which, when at Salamanca on the advance, was allowed to be the strongest English regiment ever seen in that part of the country, now reduced to a number insufficient to form a parade, and that too without firing a shot. The churchyard was now a more common resort for them; for we buried from seventy to eighty men in this town in little more than a month,—a proof how many more are killed by privations and hardships of a long campaign, than by the violence of the sword.

Severe, indeed, were our sufferings: in many instances the feet and legs of the men swelled, then turned black, gradually decayed, and finally dropped off. I will not enlarge on this unpleasant subject, which cannot, I am sure, be agreeable to the reader; I shall only observe, that I was in a very sickly state myself, labouring under violent dysentery, which had now become a chronic complaint. Most of the officers were in the same unfortunate condition, and many of them died. Fortunate, indeed, was he, who, escaping all the vicissitudes and changes of this eventful scene, has been enabled to enjoy the remainder of his life in his domestic circle!—a blessing which I conceive not to have fallen to the lot of more than one in ten of those who went through the Peninsular campaigns. It is true, I have escaped with life; but this severe dysentery, which has lasted for upwards of eight years, and other diseases, the concomitants of this long and severe campaigning, have so deranged my nervous system, as ultimately to deprive me of the sight of my left eye, and otherwise materially injure my constitution.

In this town we passed the remainder of the winter; and at length began to get the better of our afflictions, and even to muster a few men on parade. I had here a very good room with a *brazero* (a kind of grate to hold charcoal), a tolerable bed, and a very kind hostess. Time passed pretty agreeably; and more money being issued to us, we had the means of providing greater comforts. The sutlers or *huxters*, however, charging a most exorbitant price for every article, we were obliged to be extremely frugal; as experience had taught us, on the last campaign, to endeavour to provide better for the ensuing, which was ere long to commence with all the vigour of the former one, and which might probably be found as long and as eventful as any that had preceded it.

About this time a very unpleasant circumstance occurred in my habitation. My poor landlady, a widow with a large family, a very good humane creature, and who had paid great attention to the sick troops, at last, unfortunately, caught the fever, which carried her off in a few days, leaving her numerous orphan family destitute,—a misfortune which excited in all who knew and appreciated her benevolent character the greatest and most sincere regret.

From our long stay in this quarter, it became very difficult to obtain forage for our cattle; and we were obliged to go to so great a distance in search of it, that we were frequently out for a week together. On these excursions we had to cross the Estrella, or Starry Mountains, which are prodigiously high, and difficult to ascend; and, on descending, the animals could scarcely keep their footing, from the quantity of snow that fell here, which being sometimes thawed in the day, and afterwards frozen, rendered the declivity very slippery. Indeed, such was the difficulty of gaining the villages situated among these vast mountains, that the inhabitants informed me the French had never ventured to pay them a visit. We found the people extremely civil, always lodging and feeding the parties that went among them. On one of my rambles on this duty, I had the misfortune to lose a mule, that slipped down a precipice, and was killed. On returning we found the animal nearly devoured by wolves, which prowl about in packs on these heights. One of them stood and looked at us with great ferocity; but on coming closer it made off, just as one of the men was about loading his piece to shoot it, which I ordered him to do, being myself a very bad shot. So numerous were these creatures in this quarter, that, being pressed with hunger from the severity of the weather in the cold regions, they often descended during the night to our villages, and scratching open the graves of our recently buried men, preyed upon their flesh. Many of the inhabitants in this neighbourhood constantly ride with the skins of these animals over their saddles, by way of trophy; but never unless the rider has himself killed the wolf—otherwise they consider it usurping the honours of another.

We benefited greatly by these little journeys; getting many articles of provisions at a cheap rate from the villages to which we went, such as fowls, eggs, bacon, and a vast quantity of chestnuts, which were here so plentiful that the inhabitants made us presents of large quantities of them. The abundance of these towns may be conceived from their names, which in general referred to what they most abound in, such as Villa de Porco, Villa de Montaga, Villa de Castanos, Villa de Vino, &c—Pork Town, Butter Town, Chestnut Town, Wine Town, &c.

The regiment now began to make a respectable appearance on parade, mustering about four hundred men, besides convalescents; for this long continuance in quarters gave time for those who were left at depots to come up, the sick to recover, the men who had been overtaken on the retreat and made prisoners to escape, and join the regiment; as well as for fresh detachments from England to arrive. We once more began to wear a joyful countenance, and to enjoy some pleasure. The spring approached with hasty steps, and Nature began to appear bedecked in her fairest robes; but what most benefited us of all her gifts, was an abundant supply of green forage, which the neighbouring fields now afforded without our being obliged to go so great a distance to fetch it.

We had by this time in great measure repaired our past misfortunes; the baggage we lost had been replaced, and the cattle we left drowned in the rivers and broken down on the ground had been supplied by others. We began to assume an air of gaiety, amusing ourselves with horse-racing, shooting-parties, riding about the country, &c. The ladies of the place claimed our attention, which indeed had never been altogether dormant; but we had been unable to display our gallantry before in so jovial and entertaining a style as we now had it in our power to do, from a more free circulation of money, which enabled us to decorate the ball-room, the theatres, and the festive board. I shall not enter into detailed accounts of these various recreations enjoyed by those happy fellows who had the good fortune to survive their late disasters; but shall perform an act of duty in attempting effectually to remove a stigma which was thrown on the regiment in which I had the honour to serve, for I think it never too late to destroy an erroneous impression. To do this I must refer to our landing at Lisbon, where we disembarked with our full complement of men, and were certainly by much the strongest regiment in the country, even to the time of our reaching the capital of Spain; for we had received a detachment from home to supply the place of those left at sick-depots. In this effective state we were when the retreat commenced from Aranjuez, which is about twenty leagues beyond Madrid; and hitherto we had had a regular supply of rations, and experienced good weather; so that even through forced and harassing marches the troops had kept their ranks, although but a few weeks before they were at their ease in the finest and most pampered garrison in the world. They were for the most part mere boys, who had never before gone a long march, for the flower of our regiment had been lost on other services, particularly at Flushing; and these were not to be compared to the veteran troops who had become inured to change of climate, to hardships, and fatigue. When these young men began to feel the dampness of the wet ground, the want of their accustomed good fare and warm covering, and to continue an incessant march, each loaded with sixty rounds of ball cartridge, his knapsack, haversack, musket, blanket, canteen, accoutrements, and provisions (when these last could be obtained), how could it be matter of surprise, that we should be compelled to leave three times as many as any other corps did on the road, seeing that we were nearly treble the strength, and destitute of the advantages possessed by those regiments who had been familiarized with the arduous duties of a campaign? In consequence of this, we were reprimanded by the General of Division for the number of casualties we daily experienced: he appeared to imagine that the officers, particularly the subalterns, were deficient in their duty, and we were therefore turned out of the division for this apparent want of discipline. But I have seen these very officers do their duty on these urgent occasions in an exemplary manner: I have known them exert the greatest severity towards these unfortunate men, and even threaten them with punishment; but all to no purpose. I have also seen them employ the kindest methods, encourage them, take their muskets, knapsacks, &c, and carry them for these poor fellows; but without avail. Entirely exhausted, the unfortunate creatures lay down on the road-side and were overtaken by the enemy in such numbers, that in the course of twenty-four hours our regiment had lost from sixty to seventy men; but what was to be done in this deplorable case, more than entreaty and persuasion could effect? it was impossible to carry them on our backs, the spring-wagons and all other modes of conveyance were either too far in our front, or loaded to such a degree that, they could not receive more.

We were accordingly turned out of the division, and our commanding officer soon after placed under an arrest, for the supposed negligent conduct of this now unfortunate regiment. We were placed in the division that was considered the refuse of the army; but the sequel will show whether this very regiment, brigade, and division, were not to rank among the first, for the bravery and gallantry of their conduct. Indeed, as soon as the sufferings which brought this supposed disgrace on our regiment were made known to the Commander-in-chief, he immediately ordered our Colonel out of arrest! and gave us every facility in his power to free ourselves from these distressing calamities.

With respect to the report of numbers of our men having strayed from their battalions, and carried on a kind of plunder, by shooting the wild pigs, with which these woods are stocked, I am sorry to say it is too correct: but there are ill-disposed men in every corps; and if these men were determined to desert their companies, and pursue this occupation, how could their officers prevent it any more than they could hinder their desertion for different purposes? They had no other means than bringing them before a military tribunal, which could not then be assembled, or of the temporary one of a trial at the drum-head, by resorting to which the army might have been delayed there for a long time, and one half of them shot for mutiny,—the crime attached to those who will not obey their officers; for all our persuasions, threats, and entreaties, were now totally disregarded. Nor can this be wondered at: the men conceived that they might escape punishment for plundering, but they did not think it possible to escape starvation without acting as they did.

Let me now return to my companions in arms. In the month of April, we received instructions to hold ourselves in readiness for advancing again, and to provide ourselves with all kinds of camp equipage. We now had constant field-days to bring us again into discipline. The month of May arrived, when, with all our losses, we mustered seven hundred strong, and as fine a regiment as any that left their winter-quarters to encounter the ensuing campaign.

At length the long looked-for route arrived; and we marched from Santa Marhina, about the middle of this month, as fresh and in as good spirits as if we had never suffered by the incidents consequent on this exposed and active kind of life.

Previous to my proceeding, permit me to observe that, in relating the vast sufferings which I have so faintly described, it cannot for a moment be imagined that I attribute one particle of these misfortunes to the great Chief who commanded this persevering and enterprising army. On the contrary, they are only to be attributed to the fortune of war, which no human foresight could avert, nor any calculation obviate; and the principal reason of my attempting to delineate them is to show to Old England the true worth of her martial sons, conceiving that the greater the perils and dangers encountered by her soldiers, the greater praise will they have for surmounting them.

I shall now proceed to relate even greater undertakings, greater victories, and perhaps as great disasters, as I have already described; and, if there be any of my countrymen who have read this narrative thus far, and conceive I am not entitled to a compensation for the serious loss I have sustained in consequence of these sufferings, let them be kind enough to proceed, and I hope they will be induced to decide in my favour before they come to the conclusion of this little volume.[1]

---

1. I trust my lenient readers will pardon the expression of my feelings on this occasion, as I conceive I had been borne out in my expectation, by the strongest certificates from the most eminent oculists, under whose care and examination I have been, and who have honoured me with their names to the list of subscribers to this book. They state that "In this instance it appears to them, that the disease has entirely originated from the hardships to which Captain Wood has been exposed, and the complaints occasioned by such exposure." (continued on next page)

Be this as it may, I shall not dwell on such casualties, but endeavour to forget disappointments, and move cheerfully and pleasantly forward, conducting you smoothly through those rough and eventful scenes in which it has been my fate to be both an actor and a spectator.

Our march for the first two or three hundred miles was like a party of pleasure, in comparison to others we had encountered: we passed through a most delightful level country, abounding in all the verdant beauties of nature, and affording the greatest plenty of forage for cattle, which is the principal support to an army *en grande route*. Every thing and every countenance now wore the aspect of joy—the men singing, and telling their jocose stories, as they passed along hill and dale; till, leaving many fine towns and an open country in our rear, we came in sight of the enemy's videttes, and the next morning had to cross a rapid river, I believe the Ebro: part of the troops forded it; but most of the battalion-men were obliged to wait for the pontoons, as many of the soldiers who attempted to ford, not being tall enough, were swept away by the rapidity of the current.

We expected the French on the other side would oppose our crossing; but we were mistaken, as they withdrew on our appearance. Had they defended this wonderfully advantageous position, on high land nearly perpendicular to the water's edge, making it almost impossible to cross at any spot except where the pontoons were placed, and kept a steady fire of artillery on our working parties, and, indeed, all along our line of march on the banks of this river, they must have done great execution. We crossed, however, without opposition, in sight of our noble Commander, who was seated on a rock in company with General Lord Lynedoch. We defiled with music playing, colours flying, and bayonets glittering, which had a very imposing ef-

There is nothing to be regretted in losing a member even more than adequate to a limb in our country's cause: I suffer such a loss without a murmur; but, when I am informed by officers, and one of these of my own corps, that they have been remunerated for similar losses, incurred in the same manner, and on service of the same nature, my mind becomes agitated, and my honour concerned, to know the cause of my not receiving a similar reward: I trust, however, that this circumstance will be attributed, by my liberal countrymen, to any thing but dereliction of duty.

fect. On winding up the opposite hills, we halted on the top; and had no sooner got our meat on the fire, anxious to appease our appetites, after a long and sultry march, when we observed one of the Duke's staff running down a hill in the advance, and waving his hat to us. We understood him; and in less than ten minutes the troops were fully accoutred, and in march to the place which this officer had pointed out, leaving the fires, kettles, and dinners, to cook themselves: but the enemy finding us so much on the alert, and so quickly in position, withdrew their forces, and we betook ourselves to our old ground, where we found our rations extremely well boiled, and we were not long in demolishing them.

At some distance from this place we halted for a few days, when we were reviewed by our Commander; and a fine healthy appearance the troops made. At this review a singular occurrence happened to me: on passing by in review order, and coming to the spot of salutation, I was so engrossed with contemplating a man who had been so great a favourite of Fortune as our Commander-in-chief, that I absolutely forgot to salute him; nor did I recollect myself until I had passed him, when I stole my sword down from the support to the present, without ever coming to the recover. This circumstance, however, if observed, was not noticed by him; for great minds are generally engaged in great undertakings, and seldom affected by trifles.

We pursued our way, with good roads, good weather, good provisions, and plenty of dust, till we arrived in the environs of Vittoria, in the front of which town the enemy were posted most advantageously, and in great numbers: they certainly made a most imposing appearance as they formed their line of battle, towards which we advanced with a confident step; peals of artillery echoing through the lofty hills, as we descended their trembling slopes to gain the glorious field. We advanced through the tumultuous scene with a battery in our front, dealing out dire destruction; and halting here, as if to defy its greatest efforts, we waited the signal of attack: men and officers fell in every direction; and their wounds were most dreadful, being all inflicted with cannon-balls or shells, except that of our Colonel, who received a musket-shot in his stomach. Our front was exposed to the full range of this redoubt, and had to contend with a French regiment on the right of the battery; but after politely receiving us with a few sharp volleys, which we as politely returned, they retreated firing, and bent their course into a thicket. Towards this we advanced firing, and drove them furiously before us, till they were completely routed; and we had the satisfaction of passing over numbers whom we had laid prostrate. It was now that the hurry, bustle, and confusion of a great battle were experienced: such smoke, such noise such helter-skelter! the cries of the wounded—the groans of the dying—the shouts of the victors—the dragoons and artillery flying—dust in clouds—caps, muskets, knapsacks, strewing the ground—baggage, carriages, wagons, and carts, broken down. Such a spectacle might indeed cause the conquering army to exclaim, "Oh! what a glorious thing is battle!" but what must be the situation and feelings of the vanquished?

This scene continued, till night put an end to the bloody fray and equally bloody pursuit; when we halted, leaving Vittoria some miles in our rear. We had not had a morsel to eat the whole of this day, as we moved off our ground before the supplies had arrived: bread, indeed, we had not received for two days previously; we therefore appeased our hunger by plucking the corn from the ears, as we trampled over the fields of it with which this fine country abounds, and which was at this moment fit for the sickle. This expedient satisfied our craving wants till the action commenced, when our attention was attracted by other objects. One of my men picked up a French haversack, out of which he got a large biscuit, which he began eating most greedily without offering his comrade any part: at this instant a shell burst very near him, a splinter of which broke his leg; he hopped screaming away, and let fall the bread, which his comrade snatched up and ate, observing that it served the other right for his greediness.

At this time we were halted; and were, in some measure,

compensated for the loss of bread, by the plentiful supply we got of water, which, indeed, was a great advantage, after the heat and fatigue of the day.

We had now taken up our ground, and piled our arms, when some of the men went to the rear under various pretences, but soon returned: some with bread, brandy, fowls, and all kinds of eatables; others with dollars, doubloons, plate, and every article that could be procured from the French baggage, which we had passed, but dared not fall out of our ranks to take possession of at the time, having a more serious duty to perform than attending to plunder,—that of first beating the enemy away from it. I certainly must confess I regarded these wagons loaded and broken down with specie, over which we were obliged to drive the foe, with a wishful eye; but honour being with a soldier preferable to riches, I relinquished the latter for the former. We were, however, amply supplied with every thing that was good, by those who had the good fortune to share in the spoil. Indeed, for my own part, I could not complain, having contrived to get a very fine young horse, belonging to the Polish Lancers, which came running in my way without a rider, completely accoutred; and a handsome quilt, which I found very useful at night. Such plenty now prevailed, that I do not suppose there was a man in the field who had not a good meal that night from the stores of the enemy, which were copiously supplied with every comfort, and now came to us so very seasonably; for, although every man had not an opportunity of partaking in the plunder, yet there was so great an abundance of every necessary brought into camp, that they were enabled to share the provision with each other. We also got a most seasonable supply of those valuable articles—good shoes, taken from the French magazines. Our men had been constantly on the tramp for many weeks together, without having time or opportunity to get their old ones mended; indeed several of them had marched for the last few days barefooted. Not getting quite enough to supply all my men (having the charge of a company), I sent the remainder to exchange theirs with the dead men, many of whom were found scattered about the field with much better shoes than their living comrades had on; so that all got completely suited in this respect. We likewise obtained a good supply of salt, an article of great luxury in this part of the country, where it is very dear and scarce; and also tobacco, which could not be obtained previous to this day's victory,—a victory that crowned us with almost every desirable gift that honour and good fortune could confer.

To paint the scene that now ensued after the battle, among the troops, would be far beyond my power. Some were carousing over their spoils, others swearing at their ill-luck at not obtaining more; some dancing mad with *eau-de-vie*, others sharing doubloons, dollars, watches, gold trinkets, and other valuable articles. The more rational and feeling were talking of their suffering comrades, somewhat in the following strain:

"This was a devil of a fight surely! that was a woundy crack poor Barney got, wor'n't it, Joe?"

"Ah! but poor Bill Flint got a worse: he be laid low enough, poor fellow!"

"But what do you think of that fine young lieutenant of the grenadiers?"

"Why, dang it, his limbs be shivered to splinters: but I hope as how I shall see the brave fellow on a timber-toe some of these odd days; for he be a damn'd good officer."

"Ay! that he be; and bad luck to the French frogs, if they don't hop away too fast for us, we will pay them off for it yet: but we can't help trifles; so come along, Joe! here's to ye, and let's have the old song, *Our Lodgings Be On the Cold Ground*."

Amidst this extraordinary and novel scene, with a bottle of French brandy in one hand, some biscuit in the other, the fine large quilt thrown over me, and two fat fowls under my head, I sunk on my pillow to sleep.

Morning now came, and we rose from our verdant couch, with spirits become light as air, to continue the pursuit. Our provisions being issued, we set off, completely elevated by our late success and the defeat of the enemy. Besides their killed, wounded, and prisoners, they lost one hundred and fifty-one pieces of cannon, upwards of four hundred wagons of ammunition, all their treasure, baggage, provisions, cattle, stores, carriages, wagons loaded with bullion, magazines, horses, mules, carts; in short, every thing, to the very baton of their Field-marshal. Indeed, it was with the utmost difficulty that the ex-king Joseph himself escaped. Greater spoils than this field produced were never, I believe, witnessed by British troops in Europe, either before or since.

## Chapter 10

# The Pyrenees

*The foe, before retiring fast and far,*
*First slowlier fled, then rallied, then withstood;*
*Now flame for flame, and blood for blood, must tell*
*The tide of triumph ebbs that flow'd too well;*
*Now wrath returns to renovated strife,*
*And those who fought for conquest strike for life.*

Byron

We were now in quick pursuit, and hitherto had scarcely experienced a rainy day since we left our winter-quarters. It was at this time the height of summer, and very hot; but being inured to the climate, it made little impression on us. We continued following up the fugitive forces incessantly; and about the third day the atmosphere became sultry to an almost insupportable degree: the sky appeared overcast with portending clouds, containing a great portion of electric fluid,—the thunder was soon heard at a distance, and the storm gained on us rapidly, accompanied with the most vivid flashes of lightning; and it now broke over our heads in so dreadful and alarming a manner, as to confound us much more than the roaring of the French artillery: the drenching rain poured down on us in torrents, and the roads streamed with water. Night approaching, we struck into a thicket, the only place that could afford the least shelter from this dreadful tempest; and, in this state, we remained anxiously awaiting the dawn of day, when we with difficulty lighted fires to dry our wet and miry clothes, and warm our cold and miserable persons.

Being half-dried, we proceeded; and the sun bursting forth in all its splendour, soon re-animated our benumbed frames. On this day's march we were informed that the storm had killed an officer of the 34th regiment, and much hurt several of the men; indeed, it shook the whole army as if they were electrified—or, rather, as if they were standing on ground agitated by an earthquake.

We arrived in the neighbourhood of Pampeluna, which place the French had got possession of: a great part of the troops were therefore left to invest it, whilst my division went in pursuit of General Clausel, who had taken a different route from the main body of the French army. After much distressing and ineffectual marching, we found they had proceeded by the nearest road out of the country: we were consequently obliged to retrace our steps, and in a few days joined the main body of the army in following up the French, who were now retreating across the Pyrenees. We. ascended these mountains, with many a rugged step, over steep precipices and craggy rocks; and, after winding up these stupendous heights for days together, reached the summit. We were now in some measure compensated for our toils, by seeing those troops which had so often harassed us. at last driven into their own country; imagining that we at length had gained our object, in having effectually relieved the Spanish dominions from these hosts of locusts.

These airy regions on whose "cloud-capp'd" tops we were now encamped, we did not find the most unpleasant spot to be met with; for here we were supplied by the French smugglers with brandy and wine, as well as bread, fruit, and other necessaries. Another thing still more unexpected was, that among these mountains we found great quantities of wild cherries, plums, and apples; and the men even discovered green tobacco, probably cultivated by the mountaineers, which they made very palatable by drying it in the sun. We were, however, much inconvenienced by the thick and misty fogs that commonly encompassed these vast heights. Indeed, the clouds were on some occasions beneath us, and the sun shining on our camp, while it was raining in the enemy's, who were posted in the country below.

Here we remained some weeks, looking down on the enemy, who were in huts at a little distance in their native land. Forage became extremely scarce, and difficult to procure, all vegetation being now scorched up, so that our animals got very little to eat, except chopped furze, with which they made a very good shift to preserve life; but even this was with difficulty obtained, as I have too good reason to remember.

Being sent out one morning, very early, I travelled with my party a great distance, till at length I perceived a little village on the extreme right of our line, but far secluded in the towering mountains that extended in this direction. This being a spot which I did not conceive to be much visited by either French or English foraging parties, I expected to obtain here a good store of this necessary article: I therefore entered the place, and desired my men to search those out-buildings most likely to contain it; in which undertaking I was prevented from assisting them, for, just at this time, being subject to ague, I found a fit coming on, and was in consequence induced to ask the landlady of a petty dirty *posado*, where our mules were baiting, to permit me to lie down on a bed for about an hour.

This she consented to, but remarked that she had no room in which she could accommodate me, except one at the top of the house; however, I was thankful for any place to lay my head upon at this moment, and without ceremony was shown up a flight of narrow dark stairs, by a bonny, dirty, curly-haired lass, whose demeanour corresponded with the appearance of every thing I saw about me: still I was glad to follow her, that I might cover myself up and protect myself from the cold fit, which now began to make me tremble severely. On coming to the door, she pointed to a button, and spoke a great deal; but not one syllable did I comprehend, it being a language peculiar to the mountaineers: however, she made me understand, by placing her hand on her mouth, that I should preserve silence.

This certainly looked suspicious; nevertheless I turned the little wooden fastening, and gained admittance to a long gloomy chamber, not much unlike a loft: here were five or six common bedsteads, with a *palliasse*, a pillow, and an enormous wrapper to each, which seemed quite calculated for the hardy race of this district, who seldom take off their clothes. At the farther end of the room, on one of these beds, which was partly hid by the crossing of some beams put to prop up the roof, and which was only discernible by means of the few rays that penetrated the crevices of the tiles, lay two men, one of whom appeared to be in much bodily pain, as if he had been severely wounded; the other, from the slight glances I could catch of him, appeared a huge bearded sallow-looking fellow, whose countenance did not savour much of the milk of human kindness.

It struck me that this man had been left to take care of the sick one; and as they were conversing in a low French accent, and very reserved, I considered them to be French soldiers, who had hid themselves in this village, (which was partly in the French and partly in the Spanish territories,) particularly as I observed two muskets by their bed-side, with two grenadier-caps stuck on the top of them, and two hairy knapsacks hanging over their heads,—all which appeared like French accoutrements. However, as they did not seem hostilely inclined, I pretended to take no notice of them, but wrapping myself in the covering of the bed, I laid my head, which ached most sorely, on the pillow: at any other time I would much rather have rested it on a stone, than on a spot that had so strong an effluvia of garlic and every other obnoxious scent.

Here I remained shaking, and indeed I might say quaking, for I certainly had strong apprehension, that had I fallen asleep, these fellow house-mates of mine would not have acted so disinterestedly with me as their present manner seemed to indicate: however, after my fit had subsided, I took my departure without molesting them, conceiving them to be poor wounded devils, who at all events would only have been an encumbrance to me, had I taken them prisoners; so I left them to remain in their unenviable retreat for the present, being determined to see who they were on my return. I now found my way, by means of a savoury odour which pervaded the house, to the kitchen, whence it proceeded: here I was presented with a fine dish of *ollapodrida*[1] by the aforesaid lively curly-haired maid, whom I now found to be the cook, and also the mistress's daughter, and who had by this time cleaned and smartened herself up. This refreshment I enjoyed much, notwithstanding her former dirty appearance; and I found myself renovated exceedingly. Having finished this repast, and thanked my hostess and my pretty maid, (for I now began to admire her in spite of her late slovenly appearance,) having nothing else to offer to the latter, I thought myself in gratitude bound to embrace her, which she most cordially returned, and made me understand I should be welcome there again when I came that road.

I took my departure, and went directly in search of my party, whom I found loading their mules with Indian corn straw, which they had discovered in a deserted dwelling a long way from the village. As soon as they had completed this, we set off on our return; but as I conceived it my duty, I was determined to call at the inn, in order to ascertain who these suspicious characters were: but we had proceeded only a trifling distance, when we observed a scouting party of the enemy a little to our right, who from their manoeuvres appeared desirous of cutting us off; I therefore ordered my men to prime and load, to drive the cattle as fast as they could before them, and to keep together so as to be able to form in an instant. This precaution being strictly observed, and the French perceiving that we were perfectly on our guard and determined to resist any attack they might make, slackened their pace, which permitted us to proceed at our leisure, but we were obliged to avoid the village, towards which the enemy were bending their course; and after travelling all night, this escort arrived the next morning in safety at our camp.

We still remained in a state of suspense, which I soon found could not be of long duration. Being one day on piquet, I heard a brisk fire of musketry on my right, and on getting on higher ground (fearing a surprise) I observed the advanced

1. A species of cookery in much estimation in Spain.

brigade desperately engaged; and, to my great regret, I perceived those gallant regiments, the 50th and 71st, overpowered by numbers, falling back for support, and had the mortification of seeing the French take possession of their camp and strike their tents. However, the support they needed was most promptly afforded by my regiment, which after a hot contest was also compelled to move to the rear by alternate wings: a part, however, still kept possession of a commanding height, which the French wished to gain; and in the defence of it, our men, having expended all their ammunition, resorted to the novel expedient of throwing stones at the enemy, and in this manner preserved it till the remainder of the division arrived. I could not help remarking the determined bravery of the Brunswickers, who, as soon as they came near enough, rushed down upon the enemy like so many furies: this severe charge, and the support of other troops who now came up, arrested for the present the progress of the enemy. The evening drawing to a close, the firing gradually ceased, and both parties kept their ground; and the cessation was a scene of gloomy reflexions. This was a most sanguinary day, the bone of contention being the pass of Maya.

With the cloudy night came on a thick fog, accompanied with misty rain; and it was very dark. We were now about to suffer tremendous disasters: thank God, their duration was not longer than about five days; had they continued five more, inevitable destruction must have overtaken our troops, for, we were now about to fly in our turn, and suffer all the horrors of a repulsed army, in its worst plight;—such is the fortune of war!

Previous to quitting this gory spot, we were employed in collecting our wounded, by the sound of their piteous groans, as the foggy darkness prevented our finding them by any other means. These poor fellows were brought and laid by the fires made for that purpose. Now an order came to light more fires, to make the enemy imagine we were cooking, and meant to keep our ground; but this was mere *finesse*, for as soon as this order was executed, the word, or rather whisper, was circulated through the field, to stand to our arms, and we moved off by sections to commence this perilous retreat, leaving the wounded by the dwindling fires to the mercy of the foe: many were scattered about the bleak mountains far out of the main track, where perhaps they had a shorter period put to their existence by the hungry wolves, as several were at their last gasp when we left them; but there was no alternative. We could scarcely make our way over these unfrequented craggy wilds, and it was therefore impossible to render our comrades more assistance; and as to spring-wagons, carts, or any mode of conveyance, these were now out of the question—nothing of that kind being able to come among these mountains.

On quitting this position, the most dismal sensations took possession of our breasts. Not a voice, not a sound was heard, save the slow step and casual murmur of the dejected soldiers, intermingled with the moans and groans of the wounded. To add to these horrors, I once or twice trod, in the dark, directly upon, and fell over, a dead body, cold and naked as the clay it was stretched on.

In this state we kept moving on the whole of this sad and sorrowful night, amidst the mountains, the woods, and the rain; the ways being so deluged with mire, owing to the great number of cattle and baggage passing before us, that it was with difficulty we could wade through it. Daylight at length appeared, as we passed through the mournful town of Elisonda, leaving far in our rear the fine and romantic village of Roncesvalles.

We now took up our ground on these heights; where we had been stationed but a few minutes, when we saw our numerous enemy coming down the opposite hills, like flocks of sheep, or rather packs of hounds in full cry, making much the same noise, and at a distance much resembling them from their dress, which is a whitish frock, that they generally wear in wet weather.

They posted themselves on the ground in our front; and their audacity induced them to pitch the very tents that I have before mentioned as having been taken from us, directly in our view, by way of bravado. This was certainly very mortifying to us, particularly as we were obliged to continue retrograding. The siege of St. Sebastian was now about to be raised, and a general and precipitate retreat was enforced: we were therefore obliged to leave this bivouac, and march till we were benighted, and completely obscured in darkness and rain. So entangled were we among carts, horses, vicious mules, baggage, and artillery broken down, together with ammunition and other stores, which lined the roads, that we could not extricate ourselves from these impediments. Some lighted sticks and candles which the muleteers had with them, only added to the confusion; for we were not able to see one yard beyond the light, owing to the thick haze, which seemed to render even darkness still more dark.—Here the Colonel asked me where my men were, for I had only three with me out of forty, the strength of the company of which I had the command: I told him I did not know, as I could not see in the dark: however, he did not put me under an arrest for it, and a short time after daylight the lost sheep in question rejoined their battalion.

In this bewildered spot, many who could not stand were obliged from fatigue to sit down in the mire: to attempt going on was impossible, except by climbing over the different vehicles that lined the road. In this miserable plight, I seated myself against a tree, where weariness caused me, even amidst this bustle, mud, and riot, to fall fast asleep. My servant coming up, disturbed my repose, by presenting me with his cap full of tea, having trod in a box of it on the way: but he might as well have given me some of the mire that we were in to eat, as, at this time, there were no fires to make it, or, if there had, there was no utensil to have boiled it in, or any thing to have eaten with it; but still I felt grateful for his attention. We had, notwithstanding, one advantage here; for although the enemy were at our heels, we were not cannonaded, as they could not get their field-pieces up these acclivities in sufficient time. Moving on a few miles farther, to a more congenial spot, where some fires were lighted, near to one of them I could not but observe our brave and hardy Colonel:

*His square-turn'd joints, and strength of limb,*
*Show'd him no carpet knight so trim;*
*But in close fight a champion grim,*
*In camps a leader sage.*

He was stretched on his back sound asleep, and seemed to be in a pleasant dream, although the rain, which was mizzling fast, trickled down his weather-beaten furrowed cheeks: this, added to the appearance of his venerable snowy locks, and his projecting bristly eye-brows, and his manly Caledonian countenance, presented one of the most martial and dignified pictures that a poet could describe, or a painter depict.

We now continued I may say flying the whole of the day, without any food being issued, except half an allowance of rum, which recruited our sinking spirits. After refreshing ourselves with this and a little rest, we proceeded on the whole of the next night, descending the most rugged and dangerous precipices, and surmounting the highest hills, with indescribable fatigue. The next day, which was the fourth of this disastrous march, and during which we had scarcely tasted food, division orders were issued, whilst we halted a few hours. I well remember reading them: they were the most distressing, at the same time most feeling orders, that I ever heard, commencing somewhat in this manner:—"The General is aware of the many privations and hardships the troops have suffered during the last few days; but he assures them, that if they will bear them with patience and fortitude for another day, their wants shall be supplied," &c.

I trust the candid observer, who may refer to these orders, will pardon any error I may have committed in expressing them; as I inadvertently took no notes or memorandum when on service to assist my memory, not having then any idea of writing on this subject.

After halting a few hours we went forward, and, before night came on, reached a strong position on the heights of Pampeluna: here we found these orders fulfilled according to promise, a full portion of rations being delivered out to us—the most seasonable supply that troops so famished and harassed could possibly obtain. We now commenced boiling our kettles, and got some tea, our allowance of rum, meat, and biscuit,—the first since our retreat commenced, and which, indeed, we had hardly patience to wait the cooking of, having been about four days without a morsel to eat, except the withered leaves of the trees, which we chewed as we passed along to assuage the cravings of hunger. We had now a delicious repast, our full portion of rations, and tea, which was plentiful enough—witness my servant treading into a box of it. We were literally wallowing in luxury, which gave us such spirits, that, woe to the enemy who should dare to oppose us! We had taken up our ground on a very elevated spot, which commanded an extensive view; and I was here highly amused, just before dusk, by observing many of our soldiers run into a field between the hostile piquets, and dig with their bayonets. Soon after I saw many of the enemy do the same thing: they did not molest each other, but appeared even familiar, laughing and joking promiscuously. How strange, thought I, that these men, who tomorrow would be slaying each other, should now be so good-humouredly employed together! They were digging potatoes; and this ground, I believe, is generally, in point of honour, allowed to be neutral.

We now laid ourselves down to repose: our arms piled, and every man wrapped up in his blanket, close to the butt-end of his firelock; the enemy immediately in our front, and our piquets within half pistol-shot. In this state we remained waiting the morning's light, to witness the efforts attending another struggle for the Peninsula.

Before the day dawned, we were awakened by the fire of musketry close upon us, with an alarm that the enemy had surprised us in our camp: we started up; and, half asleep, "Fall in, Fall in! Stand to your arms! Quick, quick!" was the word, and instantly we were wheeled into line. The piquets only were engaged; but they were so near that their balls came whistling among us. Ours were directly called in, and the dazzling rays of this day's sun, peeping over the tops of the hills, displayed to our view the unfurled banners and glittering arms of the Gallic lines, which were drawn up in order of battle, waiting the attack. This day was ordained to crown the British arms with increased laurels, and to decide the fate of Spain. The enemy had intended this day to relieve the garrison of Pampeluna; and, had they succeeded in this attempt, this portion of the British army could never have witnessed the glories of Waterloo! They never could have fought at that battle—they must have shared the fate of Sir John Moore's troops, or again retired to the lines of Lisbon, or some other line of demarcation, had it not been for the consummate bravery of our soldiers on this glorious day.

The fight was already begun, and it was our turn to come in contact with the formidable foe. They were posted on a great height, and to that spot we hastened to dislodge them: here we saw the enemy in such force that we were obliged to show a front of six hundred men, when in reality we had not four; but we boldly advanced, till the shot flew as thick as a shower of hail about us, with a noise like the buzzing of bees.

This was severe fighting; as we were compelled to drive the enemy from mountain to mountain at the point of the bayonet, without the assistance of either the dragoons or the artillery.[2]

In less than ten minutes one half of my company were killed or wounded; my brother subaltern and the sergeant gone to support the colours, the ensign being shot; my corporal was knocked down, and myself severely wounded by a musket-ball: my men were now, therefore, left without even a non-commissioned officer to command them; but the brave fellows went on in line with the regiment, and in about five minutes more I had the satisfaction of seeing them carry the hill.

I cannot help comparing this scene to a gunner firing at a flock of sparrows; one-half of which, at the moment, may be seen on the ground—some kicking, some chirping, some hopping away; others panting, sighing, and dying; and such was the case with us.

2. I am informed by a Gentleman on the Staff, who was immediately near His Grace at this moment, that the Duke, seeing the corps advance so gallantly, asked what regiment it was; and when informed, replied, "Oh! let them alone; they will do their business well, I am sure!" or words to this effect.

After lying some time, I was taken to the rear and dressed; and horses or mules being sent for, as no other conveyance can pass in these mountains, I soon joined my Colonel and half-a-dozen other officers of the regiment in the same predicament, who were waiting a conveyance, and proceeded with them towards Vittoria, the depot of the wounded. It was here that I heard this brave man, who, as I before observed, was placed under an arrest in winter-quarters by the General of the Division, and who was subsequently shot in his stomach in the battle of Vittoria, then slightly wounded at the pass of Maya, and now covered with similar bleeding honours, after having his horse shot under him in this great action, exclaim, "You see, by Gad!—you see we can fight as well as the General and his division: you see, though he did turn us out of it—by Gad! you see. . . ." or some such words as these.

We now went at about four leagues a-day, which was excessively distressing, from the intense heal of the sun, and the pain we travelled in; for although it was so cold and foggy in the high regions from which we had just descended, we found it intensely hot in the level country, it being in the month of August.

While we were making the best of our way to this place, our brave conquerors of the Pyrenees were in their turn pursuing that enemy, who had so recently and tauntingly displayed their trifling capture of tents to our retiring columns, till they again chased them out of the Spanish dominions—never more to return.

Indeed, this part of the Peninsular war, I mean from the first attack at Maya to the time of the British retaking that pass, and subsequently, I think, was certainly the most arduous and enterprising duty that British troops ever performed: I do not by any means except the last campaign of Flanders; for that, with the exception of the three days' conflict, I regard as a mere party of pleasure in comparison with the affairs of the Pyrenees and the disastrous retreats of the Peninsula. The troops in Flanders were never without the Commissariat at hand, plenty of all kinds of necessaries, a general run of good weather, with the exception of two or three days, and a fine country to pass through, particularly as respected the roads; they were likewise under the most favourable circumstances,—that of following up a victory, with no privations or any great fatigue to suffer. But during this Pyrenean contest, there were few days elapsed in which we had not a partial or general engagement, with every privation and hardship; and I should suppose our losses were equal in proportion.

God forbid that I should be thought to mention the glorious field of Waterloo with envy! I am too well aware of the laurels gained by the heroes who fought there, to depreciate their merit in the least; on the contrary, I revere them: but to those officers who have fought in Spain, and who have also shared in the magnanimous victory of La Belle Alliance, I submit my ideas with confidence. They will surely admit, that the troops in the Peninsula behaved with as much bravery as those who had fought, at Waterloo; and that the important service rendered their nation by the troops in the Spanish conflict, was not inferior.

Oh! that I had had the good fortune to have been at the renowned battle of Waterloo, instead of the various actions, retreats, advances—advances and retreats again! how easily should I have gained a medal, honour, and fame!

It may appear from these remarks, that I am desirous of a reward of merit; and I will candidly confess that I should be proud of any thing that would add in the least degree to the honour of a soldier: but in this case I am speaking in a general point of view; for when I behold on the Continent the Russian, the Prussian, the Frenchman, the Spaniard, and soldiers of all nations, most of whom are decorated with these honourable badges, I certainly cannot help sighing at the scarcity of these memorable tokens of glory in a country that has made its thundering cannons sound from Pole to Pole, and has planted its numerous and victorious standards—emblems of its fame and greatness—from the Torrid to the Frigid Zone.

It is not the intrinsic value of these baubles that makes the soldier so covetous of them; for were only a part of the brass cannon that has been captured in the different actions melted down and converted to this use, it would be as dear to the breast it hung on as the purest gold: nor is it for the gaiety of the variegated ribbon dangling at the button-hole that the veteran desires it; but for the heartfelt satisfaction he would feel when retired to his peaceful abode, where he could still keep the spark of martial glory alight, by showing this badge of emulation and distinction to his children, his family, and friends,—a badge which would entitle him to say, "Merit, like this, my boys, has supported your King, your constitution, your laws, and your freedom; gain but these, and you will forever secure them."

## Chapter 11

# Into France

*To kinder skies, where gentler manners reign,*
*I turn, and France displays her bright domain.*
*Gay, sprightly land of social mirth and ease,*
*Pleased with thyself, whom all the world can please!*
*How often have I join'd thy sportive choir,*
*In dance and song beside the murm'ring Loire;*
*Where the gay grandsire, skill'd in gestic lore,*
*Has frisk'd beneath the burden of threescore!*

Goldsmith

I little thought, when leaving Vittoria, that I should have so soon to retrace my steps to that town! During a journey of about thirty leagues, my wound had been dressed but once, since the first day. Fortunately for me, on entering this depot, I met an old playfellow of mine when a boy, whom I had not seen for some years, and who had now obtained the rank of Staff-surgeon. He looked at me very hard for some time before he could recollect me, as I was dusty, dirty, and bloody; but as soon as he did, he came to me, and asked how I happened to be in such a sorry condition. I briefly acquainted him; when he desired me to come with him to his hospital, and I gladly accepted his invitation. They took me from my horse, and examined the wound, which was found much in want of dressing,—an operation that my old friend performed very tenderly, and then sent me to his billet to procure some refreshment, until I could get one prepared, which was soon done. Being removed to it, I was there confined to my bed some weeks, and went many weeks after on crutches. Here I cannot refrain from again observing the great attention shown by the people of the house, who brought me fruit, coffee, and cakes, and showed me every civility. I lived in this abode some time, forgetting all my troubles, and even enjoying some pleasure, for, my wound healing fast, I began to walk to the billiard-room, the Prada, and the Plaza, to see the bull-fights, and other places of amusement; and on finding myself sufficiently well to join my regiment, I obtained leave of the Commandant, and left this sprightly town for that purpose.

It is useless to enter into the particulars of a march of this kind, as there is nothing strange or new in coming up from the rear. I met at the respective stations with a depot, where I was supplied with rations; and pursuing my way, I came to St. Sebastian's, the ruins of which, caused by its great siege, very much astonished me, as I had never before witnessed the destructive effects of such a species of warfare.—It had been rendered little else than one continued heap of rubbish, and its wreck conferred the greatest honour on the brave fellows engaged there.

Leaving this skeleton of a town, I soon arrived at Fontarabia, a frontier town of Spain, and remained there a few days to rest my cattle after so long a march. I afterwards entered the French territories by crossing the Bidassoa, our troops having previously descended into this open and agreeable country. Here I found them cantoned in the most wretched outhouses and cabins; but, miserable as were the quarters, yet they were comfortable in comparison with being on the mountains. The enemy were in the immediate neighbourhood, consequently we were kept in continual hot water, from the alarms that every moment occurred; and at all hours of the night were we obliged to get under arms, and stand there in this cold season, waiting the light of day to be dismissed, that we might go to our habitations, which indeed were very extraordinary ones: they were situated in the country of Basquensa, in the province of Gascony, on the frontiers of France. I must here offer a few remarks on the peculiarities of the inhabitants.

********

They dress in a singular style, with a very flat cap on their heads; they have in general a short pipe in their mouths; they wear a sort of leathern jacket, and usually go without shoes or stockings, but have wooden shoes to wear occasionally; they commonly make use of stilts, with steps on them, that they may rise according to the depth of the mire they are obliged to pass through, for this country is more miry than any other I have been in. They looked very gigantic on these extraordinary helpers out of the mud, which appeared to me more likely to stick them faster in it; but I should imagine there is a gravelly or stony bottom under the surface, which prevents their sinking deep, and that the great quantity of mud is occasioned by the dust blown from the high ground in the summer season. Upon these machines they are most dexterous; and at the theatres I have seen the performers, by way of interlude, dance a country dance on them, and keep good time with the music.

Their physiognomy is also very singular; they have extremely long features, with an exceeding thin visage; but they are a manly and athletic race, and some of their females are very pretty and agreeable. I used to sit round their family fire-sides, to pass the long winter nights and endeavour to learn their language; and I amused myself, when off duty, (which by the way was very seldom), having no books, by assisting my landlady's daughters in their chief occupation—that of making turpentine rush lights. This process was very simple—merely boiling the material, taking care not to let it run over, or the house would be in flames. The task allotted me was to keep it stirring, whilst the more expert young ladies dipped in the wicks. After hanging them round the room to cool, these articles are packed up, and sold the next morning at market, at about a penny a dozen.

Their language is also peculiar to themselves, and very difficult to attain, as it has not the least affinity to either French or Spanish, although the people are situated between those two nations, but is a dialect in itself, called Basque. The few words that I could collect were very odd in their sound: as, *housquake*, a bellows; *scaragasca*, shake hands; *sketch-a-polita*, a pretty girl; *Debrainchin*, the Devil take you, &c. The names of the ladies were equally droll and romantic; but I cannot now recollect them.

Their customs and manners were as *outré* as their dress and language, and would take a history itself to describe: they were, however, a very good-natured obliging kind of folk; but at first much prejudiced against the English; being told by the French, when retreating through their country, by way of making them regard us with abhorrence, that we were cannibals, and would take great pleasure in devouring their children; that our very coats were stained with the blood of our enemies, and that we lived entirely on plunder, rapine, and destruction. They of course looked upon us with a jealous eye; but after being accustomed to us, they became quite at ease on this head, finding us as rational as themselves; and, from the good conduct and quiet behaviour of the men, we dwelt together in the greatest harmony.

These people live in a very frugal manner; commonly by toasting a bit of fat pork, which they let drop on a piece of bread, then bite it off, and let more drop, till all is consumed. Sometimes for dinner they have cabbage, oil, and garlic, boiled together; and by sopping some bread in this mixture, they appear to make an agreeable meal, of which I have frequently been happy to partake, when on different duties in this country.

********

The enemy, who now came on in earnest, compelled us to leave our snug abode, and take again to the field, even in this inclement season of the year. It was now the depth of winter, and they again commenced their old business of attacking us, so that we were obliged to march out to meet them; but they did not come to an engagement the first day, only arranging their forces for that purpose.

In the night, I was on piquet on the banks of the Nieve: a strong French one was posted on the other side, with a breastwork thrown up to protect them, my advanced sentry being within twenty yards of them, posted in a meadow without any covering. About break of day, my attention was attracted by a great noise from the French piquet; on going to learn the cause of it, I found them hallooing, and making signs to my sentry to fall back, at the same time presenting their pieces at him, and threatening to shoot him. On observing these proceedings I advanced, and demanded of the French officer what were his wishes?

He informed me that my sentry was too far in the advance: this caused me to consider what was to be done, as I dared not take him from his post without orders; but on looking about me I perceived, from the beaten path he had made on his daily walk, that the sergeant had not withdrawn him the usual number of paces at daybreak: I rectified this omission, and wished the officer of the French piquet good morning, who politely returned the compliment The reason of all this particularity I afterwards found out, seeing them retreat in about two hours' time. We went to take possession of their ground, and hailed the ferryman for that purpose, but found they had scuttled the boat; which accounted for their insisting on the sentry's retiring farther from the river, in order that he might not observe their motions: however, I was glad this affair terminated so well, as, had they commenced firing, my piquet must have stood but a poor chance in so exposed a situation, while the enemy were so very secure. But I could not help admiring the coolness of my sentry, for, although they threatened, and presented their muskets at him, still he walked backwards and forwards on his post, with as much unconcern as if nothing had been the matter.

Here let me most strongly recommend to all young officers to make themselves acquainted with foreign languages, particularly with the French, for in our profession there is no knowing of what essential service that knowledge may be.

The piquets being now called in, I marched two French soldiers prisoners to my regiment, who had deserted from the opposite piquet and delivered themselves up to me. After doing this, a general engagement took place, and a very sharply contested one it was.

It was the battle of Nivelle, in which my brigade bore no very active part, being in the reserve. We were ordered to deploy on our right, in order to counteract a movement of the French troops, which threatened this point: this manoeuvre was quickly performed, and the enemy seeing their designs frustrated, did not come on to the attack; but, as the evening was now wearing to a close, they drew off their forces, leaving us, as usual, masters of the field. After being on the alert the whole night and day, we piled our arms, and lighted fires on the ground where we stood; this was most dreadful campaigning—lying out in the open fields in this cold and wintry weather, without any covering but our blankets or cloaks.

In this bleak situation we remained, wishing most heartily for morning, preferring a contest with the enemy to perishing in the cold and damp of the night. Daylight at length came, and we waited the whole of the day, expecting the French every moment to attack us again; hut they thought better of it, so we lighted our fires, and set ourselves to work, broiling our rations on the wood-ashes, having no baggage or cooking utensils with us. At night we again cringed together round the fires: some fell asleep, some were telling stories to drown care, but most were grumbling and swearing, till a thick and drenching misty rain coming on, pretty well quieted us, and made us huddle more closely together, waiting in silent and sullen expectation the approach of light; for my part, being never of a very strong constitution, and having at this time a severe dysentery which weakened me much, I fell fast asleep, with my feet close to the fire for warmth.

I was awakened by the heat, and to my sorrow, on examination, I found I had scorched the soles of my shoes in such a manner that one of them literally fell from its upper leather. In this situation we stood to our arms; but it would have required the pencil of Hogarth to paint the figure I here cut, with a wearing disease on me, on arduous and fatiguing duty, exposed for some days to the inclemency of the most rigorous weather at this dreary season of the year, rising from my comfortless bed, and falling shivering into the ranks, with my cap, which had served me both for pillow and nightcap, crushed into different forms, my beard somewhat grown, my eyes sunk in, my cheeks quite hollow, my frame diseased and filthy, my countenance woeful, my shoes without a sole, my sword, from having been drawn all day and sheathed in a wet scabbard at night, covered with rust, my belt of a deep brown, my epaulette very blue, my shirt very black, and my coat any colour but red, and in the most wet and miry condition: had I been transported from this unhappy spot by some magic hand, and placed on the centre arch of London Bridge, I should have filled more hearts with pity and compassion than any mendicant of this great metropolis. It was now that the fine uniform I mounted in Lewes Barracks made the appearance I before hinted it would ere long be subject to.

The enemy, however, still forbore to attack us; indeed, such was the bad state of the weather, that they, like us, were unable to keep the field, and we received orders to move off to our respective cantonments,—most joyful news for us! We arrived late in the evening at our quarters, where we soon made ourselves comfortable by a good fire, this country abounding in fuel; and after taking some refreshment, I soon got into a comfortable bed, and drowned all my miseries in sleep.

We had now a little respite, owing to the badness of the weather, attending only to the common routine of duty, as guards, piquets, foraging, &c. In this suspense we remained for a short time, but on Christmas day, just as we were about to make ourselves as jovial as circumstances would permit, and drink a good health to all our good friends in Old England, the drum beat to arms. We immediately fell in, and left our roast beef and plum-pudding (for we had exerted ourselves much on this occasion to procure so grand a dinner), and again marched to bivouac in the open fields, which we kept for several days, observing the motions of the enemy, which wore a threatening aspect.

On one of these mornings, as my comrade and I were reclining on the side of a rocky mountain, the sun just breaking through the frosty horizon, and the enemy appearing, moving in the glittering attire of martial array, I jocosely observed to him,

"See what a glorious life we warriors lead, what honour and renown we acquire! surely, from this experience we shall become second Hannibals!"

"D—n your honours and your Hannibals!" said he; "give me a good leg of mutton and a snug little cot, and I would gladly resign to you warriors this honour, fame, and glory, with every kind of success attending it."

This poor fellow lost his life afterwards by shipwreck, going with his regiment to his native country, Ireland, after surmounting all the difficulties of several campaigns.

We were now ordered to change our position, and remain a few days longer in the field, going through much the same kind of unpleasant duty as formerly, the particulars of which I am afraid I have been already too tedious in detailing.

During the remainder of the time we continued out we had the advantage of fine weather, the nights being clear and moonlight, though very cold; and we enjoyed a regular supply of provisions, the sea-ports on the coast being open to our shipping.

The bad weather soon began to set in, which drove us again into our cantonments, where my complaint increasing, and my wound breaking out afresh, I was confined to my quarters. At this time an order came to advance; but not being well enough to proceed immediately with the regiment, I remained in the house of my French host. I was now in an enemy's country; yet for the politeness, care, and tenderness of these people, I must ever feel the sincerest gratitude.

## CHAPTER 12

# Bayonne & the End

*The hardy veteran, mark'd with many a scar,*
*Leans on his sword to take a farewell view,*
*And sighing, bids the glorious camp, adieu!*

Tickell

My regiment having departed, I was obliged to go to a depot for medical assistance, where I remained for some weeks. At length I began to gain strength; and on looking one day at the Gazette, I had the satisfaction of seeing myself promoted to a company, soon after which I proceeded to join my regiment. I passed over the floating bridge of ships across the Adour, and halted for the night in the immediate neighbourhood of Bayonne, when, about three in the morning, I was awakened by a tremendous fire of small arms, with a heavy gun at intervals: I directly got up; and going to the spot, had a fine view of the famous sortie made from that fortress; but being an individual, I could not take an active part—nor was there any occasion, for I soon had the gratification of seeing our brave troops drive in the enemy to their strong garrison; though they suffered here a great loss, and their Commandant, General Sir John Hope, was taken prisoner—in consequence of his horse having been shot under him, and its rider being so entangled in its fall that he could not escape.

The success of our forces seemed to reanimate my spirits, and I continued my route daily through the forests of pine-trees, so numerous in this part of the country. I observed the process by which they obtained the turpentine from them, of which they make most of their candles in the neighbouring towns. It is sufficiently simple: it consists in merely digging a small hole at the foot of the tree, and then cutting streaks in the bark, by which the turpentine is conducted to it, and thus they take it out with little more trouble.

In a few days I arrived at Dax, a fine town, famous for a great phenomenon, which I cannot pass without noticing—I mean a pond of very considerable size, as clear as crystal, and perpetually on the boil: I could plainly see to the bottom, though it was in a state of constant fermentation, and had in every respect the appearance of a copper of boiling water, bubbling up and steaming in the same manner. Though I saw every symptom of this large sheet of water being very hot, I could not believe it without sensible demonstration: I therefore put my finger into it; but was instantly forced to draw it out again—it being as much scalded as if I had put it into an utensil of the same liquid boiling on the fire.

I was informed that the inhabitants on the spot make use of it on all requisite occasions: it certainly is very convenient, and saves them the expense of fuel, as they can make their chocolate with it, or boil an egg in three minutes.

On leaving this town, every day brought me into a more beautiful country. I now met thousands of the army lately under the command of the *ci-devant* Emperor, the greater part of whom had laid down their arms since his defeat by the northern Allies, and were dispersing to their different homes. They were composed of the most singular medley of nations; French, Corsicans, Portuguese, Italians, Spaniards, &c. who had been forced into his service. Some of these were desperate-looking characters, and had committed all kinds of robberies and depredations on the road; this part of the kingdom being at that time infested with brigands, which made it very unpleasant and dangerous to travellers. These hordes of ragamuffins were constantly passing me, but I was never molested by them: I suppose my cloth again protected me, and that they thought every one of the profession as poor as themselves. I jogged on very leisurely through this charming country—an armistice having taken place between the contending forces.

As I proceeded, I was overtaken by a French nobleman and his servant: the former bore on his breast a Cross of St. Lewis, which he afterwards informed me he had not worn externally for the last twenty years, although he had constantly carried it next his heart. On coming up to him, he politely accosted me, and asked the particulars of the late sortie at Bayonne: I made him understand what I knew of the affair but indifferently; for, although I could comprehend the language tolerably well, yet for want of practice I could not speak it fluently; but he very kindly assisted me, instead of laughing at the attempt of a foreigner to make himself understood, as I have so frequently seen done in my own country.

He afterwards requested that I would do him the honour of dining with him, and halting at the same inn for the night. My route did not specify my stopping at this town; but I gladly accepted his kind invitation, and a most excellent dinner we had, with the choicest wines. I shall not mention the different delicacies that were served up; but among them was a dish somewhat resembling stewed larks, and after my dinner was nearly finished, the Chevalier taking up the dish said, *"Monsieur, voulez-vous prendre un petit morceau defricassée de grénouilles."*

I recollected immediately the name of frog, and out of pure curiosity took some, which I found very palatable; but, from the natural antipathy an Englishman has to these animals, I did not neglect to wash them down with a bumper of good wine, the more effectually to do away with any disagreeable sensation.

We met with excellent accommodation at this inn, and the next day, after breakfast, our servants having brought our horses to the door, we travelled along together very pleasantly. It being now the spring of the year, the hawthorn had begun to blossom, the vineyards were already decked in their greenest attire, as well as the Champaign fields and flowery meadows; the little choristers warbled incessantly wherever we passed, and all nature appeared in her gayest colours. The robust peasants, with the comely healthy country lasses, were toiling in the fields and tending their flocks. These pleasing objects formed a picture that even our very horses appeared to enjoy.

We heard, too, that sweet little messenger of spring, the nightingale, which my fellow-traveller remarking, exclaimed, *"Le voilà, Monsieur le Capitaine, entendez-vous le musicien du bois?"*

In this agreeable manner we went on, conversing on different topics; and he informed me that he was going to Bourdeaux to visit his daughter, who was married to a gentleman of that city. He said, that if I would do him the pleasure of accompanying him thither on a visit, every attention should be shown me: this kind offer I told him my duty prevented my accepting, as I was on my way to join my regiment, which was stationed at Langon, about three days' journey, through which place he must pass, as it was on the high road. He asked me what regiment it was; I informed him it was *"le Regiment de Volontaires du Prince de Galles."*

*"Ah! ma fois!"* said he, *"il faut que je voie ce brave régiment"*

I replied, that I should have great pride in showing them to him; and on my arrival, after breakfast, as they were then on parade, I accompanied him thither. Not having seen an English regiment before, he appeared very much pleased with their appearance, particularly with the band, which was always in great repute; and he was very familiar with the officers to whom I introduced him. He observed that in point of our numbers he was much disappointed. I informed him, that when we first landed we were upwards of a thousand strong, but that his countrymen and the fortune of war had reduced us to the number he then saw. He shook his head and exclaimed, *"Mon Dieu! telle est la fortune de la guerre!"*

On our return he very affectionately took leave of me, and requested that if I ever came to Bourdeaux, I would consider his son's house my home. So saying, he bade me a friendly *adieu*.

Some time after this we received orders to proceed to that city, where we went into quarters. I very much regretted not being able to wait on my agreeable travelling-companion, having lost his address. Indeed, I suppose he had returned into the country, as I never met him after.

We remained some time in this gay town, which was indeed a different scene to what we had been accustomed to. Here were amusements of every kind to be met with; elegant theatres, operas, assemblies, fine public walks, and parks adorned with beautiful females of exquisite symmetry, promenading with the most graceful deportment. To an agreeable and fascinating air, they joined great vivacity, piercing sparkling eyes, and much animation of countenance; in fact, most of them are charming pretty women.

From the length of time I had now been on active service, my health was much impaired; and it was thought necessary by the Physician of the Forces that I should go to England; particularly as I no longer belonged to this battalion, my promotion transferring me to another. I therefore waited a passage for that purpose; and being now convalescent, began to enjoy the fine walks about this delightful town. My appetite also improved, and was easily gratified by the choice collection of every thing rare which this abundant place produced.

A wonderful change was also perceptible in the countenances of the men, who had so lately had the appearance of famine, dejection, and fatigue, from their late sufferings. Their countenances were now beaming with health and content, for this was a most excellent quarter: the finest fat beef, fed on the luxuriant pastures of the fertile meadows which border the lively Garonne, was here to be had for about twopence per pound; bread, wine, fruit, and every article of life in proportion, except tea and sugar, which were imported in a great measure from England. Our troops, living on this kind of fare, regained their natural ruddy, robust, and soldier-like appearance. The sick and wounded now recovering, and fresh detachments arriving, increased our regiment so much, that it again became one of the strongest in this country; it was consequently one of the first ordered to embark for America,—an unlucky order, for it deprived us of sharing in the honour of the battle of Waterloo; but I think we may boast of this consolation, that our generous country gives equal praise to her troops, wherever they gallantly distinguish themselves.

For this service we were allowed a considerable time to prepare; which interval we passed very pleasantly, living in the most sumptuous style. For about half-a-guinea a-day we got, at the first inns in the town, a sumptuous dinner, with champagne, claret, and all kinds of rich wines, as well as an excellent dessert; after which we generally went to the play, the opera, a ball, or to some private party; for the gentry of the town took great pleasure in paying the most marked respect to the English officers, and showed them all imaginable civility. The ladies, in particular, were exceedingly attentive and affable; so much so, that they made a strong impression upon the hearts of our young sparks, and one of our officers was fortunate enough to make a lovely damsel in this neighbourhood the partner of his life. There are moments of happiness, to cheer even the heart of the wandering soldier! but so capricious is Fortune to the sons of war, that this dashing gallant indulged but a very short time in the charms of his amiable spouse; he was ordered to embark two days after, and his disconsolate bride was obliged to wait with impatient anxiety the return of the object of her affections from an American campaign.

So very engaging and agreeable are the charming young ladies of this town, that I may with truth assert, nearly the whole of the officers had in a great measure lost their hearts: even in the married ones, it required the greatest constancy and resolution to retain their attachment for their affectionate wives at home; and so deeply were many of the bachelors in love, that, had not a sudden order snatched them from this paradise of fascinating female society, many more would, I have no doubt, soon have sacrificed at the nuptial shrine; but love, however powerful, must yield, though reluctantly, to the imperative call of war!

In this routine of pleasure, time flew quickly away. The regiment embarked for its destination in the New World, and I proceeded to Old England to join another battalion; but it was with the greatest regret I left this fine corps, in which I had seen so many arduous but glorious days.

After remaining at anchor in the roads some days, we set sail for our different destinations. We were favoured with a fair breeze, and my heart was full of joy at the prospect of again seeing my country and friends, after so long an absence, attended with such constant hardships, difficulties, and anxiety of mind. But though these agreeable sensations occupied my mind almost entirely, I felt some regret at leaving a country with which I had now become familiar, and where I had experienced content and happiness, from the kindness and friendship I had met with in it, which even counterbalanced the discomfitures I had suffered.

We had just come into soundings, when the fine wind changed into a gale directly against us, so that we could not lay our course; and it ultimately drove us into the Bay, by me so much dreaded from the furious storm with which I had to contend there on my first going out. I was apprehensive of a repetition on my return; which, indeed, proved the case: but I shall not trespass on the patience of the reader, by again entering into particulars similar to those stated in the early part of this Narrative. We sustained all the violence and fury of the hurricane with patience; for experience, among other desirable acquisitions, teaches us this great one. The wind at last favoured us, and we bore away for the Channel, made land the day after, and the next day disembarked at Plymouth.

I was not yet recovered from the effects of the late storm; but being determined to make myself as comfortable as possible, I put up at the principal hotel: I immediately called for the landlord, to know what was the best fare the larder afforded for supper: he answered, any thing I might please to order. I at once recognised in his reply English accommodation, which is certainly the best in the world, although the best price must be paid for it, as I found out in the morning, before taking my departure from the town.

On arriving at Bath, I found the action of the ship not yet out of my head; the confusion of my brain was such, that, although sitting still, I fancied myself in perpetual motion. I therefore found it necessary to remain all night; and, to drown ennui and make myself at ease, to order something reviving. I called the waiter, and desired him to get. me as quickly as possible for dinner some veal cutlets, ham, and green peas. At the mention of this last article, he looked at me very hard: "Sir!" said he.

"Get me some veal cutlets and green peas," said I.

"I can procure you some green peas, Sir; but they are half-a-guinea a quart!" This answer made me stare in my turn.

"Why!" replied I, "I have had them in plenty at Bourdeaux for the last fortnight."

"That may be, Sir, but they are not to be had here in such plenty at present."

"Then," answered I, "you must entertain me in the best manner you can; I will leave things entirely to you and the chambermaid."

A very good accommodation I had: but I could not but reflect on the very great difference a few leagues made in climate;—Bath not having the same vegetables fit for the table for at least three weeks after they had been plentiful in Bourdeaux; and one quart of green peas, at the former place, costing as much as the Champagne wine, dinner, dessert, and all the luxuries of the table put together, had done at the latter. In point of economy, the South of France is certainly a most desirable residence.

The next day I set off for London, where I arrived in a very reduced state of health. I remained some time in the capital, as I was obliged to undergo a complete refit, in order to join the 2nd Battalion. My campaigning uniform was so completely tattered, that I was compelled to throw it out of the window at Bourdeaux, and dress myself in plain clothes for travelling in, which I procured in that town, made in the most stylish and fashionable manner. As it was then almost a novelty to appear in London with a French dress, the tailors and shoemakers solicited the inspection of my apparel as a most finished cut; indeed, the boots made at Bourdeaux are certainly the neatest I ever saw, not excepting those made in Bond Street. Every kind of trinket may also be procured there very cheap, such as watches, rings, brooches, &c. They appear at first sight very beautiful, and of exquisite workmanship; but, on wearing them a short time, they are found to be so flimsily put together, that it is far better to purchase substantial articles of this kind in England, which, though at a higher price, will in the end be found the cheapest, to say nothing of running no risk of losing them by the officers of the Revenue.

Having completed my re-equipment, I proceeded to join my regiment, which was stationed at Alderney. This diminutive island is only seven miles in circumference; but little places and little persons I have commonly found the most agreeable, and so it was here. The quarters were exceedingly pleasant and comfortable, and we received every attention both from the civil and military Governors. Here we were stationed some time looking at the enemy's coast, which had again become hostile, owing to the Corsican's escape from Elba. This was the means of keeping us much on the alert here; the Commandant of this small fortress being aware of the local importance of this little island. It was formerly famous for the retreat it afforded to smugglers; at present it is principally celebrated for its very fine breed of pretty little dairy cows, which are here so productive that they are milked three times a day, and afford perhaps the most delicious butter in the world. Every precaution was taken to defend it in case of an attack, and the most judicious arrangements were made, which kept our little garrison in the greatest order and most active state of discipline: in this respect, indeed, it might rank in miniature with the great fortress of Gibraltar.

This island, although so small, possesses very great advantages: its situation is healthy, its scenery beautiful, and its appearance romantic. Great taste has been displayed in the improvements made by its Governor, Colonel le Mesurier, and in the spring of the year I hardly know a more enchanting spot; the vegetation is nearly equal in point of quickness and luxuriousness to that of the neighbouring shore, which is easily seen from what is here called the Bley—a large piece of ground, of about five hundred acres, divided into an immense number of parcels, occupied by the different inhabitants, and sown with various kinds of vegetables. Thus this spot has almost the appearance of a quilt made of patchwork, so variegated is the face of its beautiful enclosure. In harvest it retains the same form, but with different colours: from various shades of green, they are now transformed into the most beautiful bright colours of yellow and green intermixed. From this place there is a delightful view of the French coast opposite; and the inhabitants may clearly be seen, by the help of a tolerable glass, tending their flocks. This prospect renders the fields here very pleasing walks, but not very shady, there being but few trees on the island.

On this large and well cultivated piece of ground the worthy Governor, at the conclusion of the harvest, gives annually a most sumptuous entertainment to the inhabitants and the military, which is extremely inviting. The society you meet with is agreeable; a full band of music attends, and the beauty of the surrounding scenery is enhanced by the natural sprightliness of the peasant lads and lasses who resort to this rendezvous of mirth and jollity, which not a little resembles a country fair.

With respect to the amiable qualities of the females belonging to the higher classes in this pleasant island, there is reason to say everything complimentary. Alderney may justly be compared to the Island of Calypso; and the attractions of these fair damsels is even more potent than hers, for should any gallant get entangled in the snares of love here, it is almost impossible for him to extricate himself. This no less than five of my brother-officers who were quartered in this fascinating place can testify, having each married one of the fair residents: and which indeed is not to be wondered at; for where young gentlemen experience attention, respect, and friendship, it is very natural that they should, in return, be induced to share their heart, love, and fortune, with such engaging and endearing objects; and were this condescension a little more practised in England, I am of opinion that the female part of society would be materially benefited.

When I remark that it is impossible for a gentleman to extricate himself if he fall in love in this island, I do not mean to infer that he is entangled like a bird in a net; but should he quit the island without marrying the object of his attachment, he is obliged to return and complete his courtship by marriage. This is owing to a strange practice prevalent in these islands, which is called flouncing; and when this, which is nothing more than keeping each other company, takes place, it is held as sacred as a marriage-contract: thus, if once a gentleman is flounced, or engaged to a lady, she never by any chance thinks of another object of affection, but implicitly relies on her gallant's honour, which is rarely, if ever, forfeited.

Although this colony is very small, yet, besides the land cultivated on the Bley, it has an extensive commonage, on which a great many of their young cows are reared. Upon the whole, this pretty little island is a very desirable quarter, and in every respect calculated for a pleasant summer residence. I consider it one of the most unique retirements in the British dominions.

Time, stealing quickly on, removed us from this spot; for it is commonly the case, in our restless profession, too soon to quit the place in which we are most desirous to remain. The route came, and we embarked by detachments in a small vessel for Guernsey, where transports soon arrived and conveyed us to Portsmouth, at which place we disembarked and went into barracks. We remained in them but a few days, when we marched for Winchester, which town I anticipated great pleasure in seeing, from having heard that it was the place of my nativity; but I did not observe anything peculiarly attractive or extraordinary in that ancient city, which we left a few weeks afterwards, and proceeded to Fort Monkton—our final destination.

After remaining there some weeks, the death-warrant of our regimental existence was at last signed, and we were with very little preamble released from our long and arduous duties. Peace had been proclaimed with all the world, and there was no farther occasion for our services. Being now my own master, not subject to orders, reprimands, or martial law, I found myself as light as a bird that has had the door of its cage thrown open and been set at liberty. Oh! happy Liberty! at thy shrine let me offer up my devotions for all thy favours conferred upon me. I have no longer different climes to contend with, nor hardships, storms, or dangers, to encounter; and living in thy happy land, at my own free will and pleasure, envying no man's wealth, but perfectly satisfied with the liberal allowance of Government for my trifling services, there is nothing that would induce me to quit this free State, but the honour of again serving my King and my Country!

# A Brief History of the 82nd Regiment in the Age of Napoleon

82nd. Regiment of Foot

# The Eighty-Second Regiment in the Age of Napoleon

The 82nd Regiment was chiefly recruited in the counties of York, Lancaster, Lincoln, Stafford, and Worcester. It was placed on the establishment of the Army from the 27th September, 1793, and was stationed at Stamford in December of that year.

By the special permission of His late Majesty King George IV., then Prince of Wales, the distinctive appellation of The Prince of Wales's Volunteers was accorded to it, at the solicitation of its first colonel, Major-General Leigh, a gentleman of the Prince's household. This permission was confirmed by King William IV., on the 20th December, 1831, under his sign-manual, of which the following is a copy:

> 82nd Regiment to retain the title of Prince of Wales's Volunteers in addition to its number, and also to bear the Prince of Wales's Plume on the regimental colour and appointments.
> (Signed) *W. R.*

In February, 1794, the regiment, consisting of ten companies, marched from Stamford to Newbury and Basingstoke; and in April, mustering one thousand men, it marched to Windsor, under command of Lieutenant-Colonel Garnier, and continued to do duty there and at Hampton Court for four months. On the 31st August it embarked at Southampton for Gibraltar.

At this time the National Convention of France had appointed commissioners to stir up an insurrection in St. Domingo; and Brissot, the leader of the party, who was accused of having advised the measure, suffered an ignominious death. These civil commissioners were looked upon as the cause of the total ruin of the island. The unhappy state of France rendered it incapable of sending succour to this ill-fated country, and many of the most respectable proprietors of St. Domingo were forced to apply to England for protection, which was granted them. The following curious correspondence took place between the English and French commanders. Colonel John Whitelocke, who commanded one of the expeditions, and acted as Deputy Quartermaster-General to one of them, addressed a letter to Lavaux, the French Governor-General at Port de Paix, offering him the same protection as had been granted to the proprietors of the island, on condition that he should first deliver the town and forts of Port de Paix and its dependencies into the possession of the British Government; which being complied with, the officers and soldiers under Lavaux's command would enjoy the same favours as had been granted to those of the Mole; and fifty thousand crowns were offered to him personally on his delivering the forts into the hands of the officer appointed to receive them. Colonel Whitelocke went on to say, that His Britannic Majesty intended to use the most vigorous efforts to take possession of the island of St. Domingo, or of that part of it not yet subdued by the arms of Spain, and that he was in hourly expectation of considerable forces from England.

The French General replied, that all the forces with which he was threatened could not shake his courage. Like the three hundred Lacedemonians who all died at their post, he and his men would defend their station to the last, and sell their lives as dearly as they could. He complained of the indignity offered to himself in thinking him so vile, so flagitious, so base, as not to resent an offer of fifty thousand crowns. Hitherto he had been worthy to command his army. Colonel Whitelocke had endeavoured to dishonour him in the eyes of his comrades, and he demanded satisfaction in the name of honour, which must exist between nations. Therefore, previous to any general action, he offered the English Colonel single combat until one of them should fell, leaving the choice of arms to his adversary, either on foot or on horseback. He concluded thus:

> Your quality of enemy, in the name of your nation, did not give you a right to offer me a personal insult. As a private person I ask satisfaction for an injury done me by an individual. Our two nations have often made war with each other, but always with equal weapons. Cease then to attack us by tenders of money. Let us be equally generous, let us contend in honourable hostility, and let us scorn the arts of seduction. I invite you to read my letter publicly, as it is written in public. I greet you in the name of the whole army.
> *E. Lavaux*

A second battalion of the 82nd Regiment was raised by authority dated 12th March, 1794, which was sent to Jersey, and remained there until 20th April, 1795, when it likewise embarked for Gibraltar, six hundred and sixty-three rank and file, under command of Captain Walter Strickland; and continued to form a portion of this garrison until December, 1795, when it was reduced, and the men drafted to other corps. The first battalion embarked eight hundred and forty-four rank and file at Gibraltar for St. Domingo, under command of Lieutenant-Colonel Garnier, on the 10th June, 1795, after giving over certain men to the second battalion.

On reaching Cape St. Nicholas Mole, in St. Domingo, it was immediately despatched to Port-au-Prince, the seat of Government, where the garrison was much reduced by sickness, and the place was threatened with an assault. The timely arrival of nearly one thousand Europeans placed Port-au-Prince in a state of security, and enabled Major-General Sir Adam Williamson, K.B. to commence offensive operations. Three hundred men, in three companies, were at once marched, under Major Tinker, with a strong body of colonial troops, to dislodge the enemy from the district of the Grand Bois; and this was the first occasion on which the 82nd was opposed to an enemy. The object was effected with *éclat*. Major Tinker was wounded, and afterwards died of his wound on his passage to America. After dislodging the enemy from the district of the Mirebalais, as well as from the Grand-Bois, the three companies remained on the frontier of the Spanish portion of the island, and were joined by the other seven companies, which had been detached amongst the posts of most importance and had become much reduced in numbers. At the instigation of the French Republic war had been declared by Spain against Great Britain. The Island of St. Domingo was now in the power of the negroes, but the French were in possession of a small part of it, and a British force having occupied Port-au-Prince, constant warfare was carried on between them. The flank companies of the 82nd, while forming part of the garrison of Port-au-Prince, were engaged in a sortie made by Lieutenant-Colonel Garnier, who was wounded. While in the district of Mirebalais, during twelve months, being the only European troops in that district, they had in conjunction with the Colonial levies repelled several attacks of the enemy. The frequent marches and counter-marches, and continued exposure by day and by night, very much harassed the men, who suffered many privations, and were for a considerable time without shoes. During this period of activity and hardship the corps remained comparatively healthy, and though it must be presumed that many casualties occurred, the only loss recorded is that of Lieutenant White, who was wounded, and four men killed.

The most serious of these attacks was made by the black chief, Toussaint L'Ouverture, on the whole line of frontier, when forty men of the 82nd, under Lieutenants Manners and Conyers, accompanied by two thousand five hundred Colonial troops, marched at night to assist Fort Serolle, then invested by four thousand of the enemy, who were surprised, dislodged and dispersed, with considerable loss.

By the temporary cessation of the attacks the regiment was left in a state of quiet, but the ravages of disease in this fatal climate soon reduced it to a skeleton.

In November, 1796, it was ordered to Port-au-Prince, and embarked for Jeremie, and landed there considerably under one hundred of all ranks, after a residence in the island of but fourteen months. The muster roll is dated Jeremie, 18th November, 1796, and even included some officers recently joined from England.

An old order to draft the men was now acted on, though the number so disposed of did not amount to twenty; and from this period the record of the regiment dwindles into little more than a journal of the few individuals who escaped the fate of their comrades. But, however few their numbers, they constituted the corps.

In 1797 the surviving officers, each with a few non-commissioned officers attached to him, were dispersed to act with other corps at the different forts and stations.

The colours were sent to Port-du-Centre, with Captain Bingham, who commanded the post.

Lieutenant Talbot was detached to Fort Irois, which was suddenly and unexpectedly attacked by night, on the 20th April, 1797, while the chief part of the garrison were in the bourg below. Lieutenant Talbot gallantly defended the place with a few men of the 17th Regiment, and about twenty Colonial artillerymen. He was killed, and some of the non-commissioned officers with him were wounded.

The attack was repeated thrice and was thrice gallantly repulsed, until the defenders were reinforced by three hundred and fifty men of Prince Edward's Black Chasseurs, and the enemy was finally driven off, with a loss of one thousand men.

From Brigadier-General George Churchill
To Lieutenant-General Simcoe
Commanding in St Domingo
Our loss was trifling indeed, consisting only of three privates killed; but I have to lament Lieutenant Talbot, of the 82nd Regiment, an officer of the most extraordinary bravery and good conduct, and Lieutenant Colville, of the Black Chasseurs, the only persons wounded, and since dead.

Lieutenant Conyers commanded Fort Desureaux, with a garrison of forty Europeans and three hundred Colonial troops. He had to repel several assaults, and when Pestel was attacked he led a party against the rear of the enemy, which caused the failure of their enterprise, and for his conduct on this occasion he received a letter of thanks from Brigadier-General Churchill.

In November, 1797, the Brigadier-General collected his whole disposable force, amounting to four thousand Colonial troops and fifty Europeans, to repel these constant inroads. The command of the Europeans was given to Lieutenant Conyers, 82nd, who had with him Lieutenant Tubb and eight non-commissioned officers of his regiment. This force marched through the woods to surprise the enemy's stronghold at L'Ance-a-Veaux, but failed and was obliged to retreat to Pestel, where reinforcements being added, a more determined attack was made by sea. This also failed, with considerable loss, a portion of which fell upon the small number of the 82nd employed.

In March, 1798, Lieutenant Conyers was appointed Fort-Major of Irois, and proceeded thither with a few non-commissioned officers of the corps, previous to the third investment of that fort. The siege continued three months, during which time the garrison lost more men killed and wounded than its original number of three hundred. Lieutenant Conyers and two non-commissioned officers of the 82nd were wounded, and during the siege Sergeant Shaw, 82nd, distinguished himself by taking upon his head and throwing over the parapet a live shell which fell at the door of a temporary and ill-constructed magazine.

Towards the end of 1798 treaties were made with the hostile chiefs for the evacuation of the island, and the remains of the 82nd were collected at Jeremie, under command of Lieutenant Conyers, the only remaining officer of the original number who less than three years before landed at St. Domingo.

On the 1st November, 1798, the battalion mustered six officers, twenty-two sergeants, and ten rank and file.

After the successive evacuations of Jeremie and Cape St Nicholas in September and October, 1798, the regiment proceeded to Jamaica.

The Island of St. Domingo was totally evacuated by the British in March, 1799, in pursuance of a suspension of arms entered into by Brigadier Thomas Maitland, and by the end of the year the French likewise withdrew their troops, so that the negro chief, Toussaint, remained in possession of the principal authority of the entire island without further fighting.

The 82nd landed at Gravesend on 27th January, 1799, twenty-four effectives (sergeants and drummers), who marched to Chatham and joined about one hundred recruits and volunteers from reduced corps.

The total loss of the regiment in St. Domingo was twenty-two officers (the precise number which embarked at Gibraltar) and one thousand men.

On the 5th March, 1799, the regiment marched from Chatham to Kidderminster under Lieutenant-Colonel Coghlan, where it arrived on the 19th of the same month.

On the 13th July, it marched for Ealing Barracks, near Southampton, arriving there on the 30th July, and was then recruited to eight hundred men, by volunteers from the East York, Shropshire, East Somerset, West Middlesex, and West Kent Militia.

On the 13th January, 1800, it marched from Southampton to Portsmouth, and embarked on the 16th for Ireland, reaching Cork and Kinsale about the 18th February, after a stormy and dangerous voyage of five weeks. It marched immediately to Fermoy, and occupied temporary barracks at that place.

********

Before following the regiment again on foreign service, it will be necessary to notice briefly the state of affairs on the Continent of Europe, where General Bonaparte was looked upon by his own countrymen with confidence and admiration, and by his enemies with doubt and fear.

In July, 1798, he had landed with an army in Egypt, and occupied Alexandria and Cairo, where he was completely isolated from Europe; but when the Directory of France became embarrassed after the Battle of Novi and capture of Mantua by the Austrians, they thought of General Bonaparte, and invited him to give up his command in Egypt and return to France. He accepted the invitation, and landed at Frejus on the 9th October, 1799.

On Christmas Day, 1799, Napoleon, who had been elected First Consul of France, addressed a letter to the King of Great Britain, asking " whether war must be eternal, and whether there existed no means of coming to an amicable understanding."

The British Government refused to appoint a plenipotentiary, on the principle of non-intervention, but, in reality, upon disapprobation of French aggression on the States allied to England. On this refusal, Napoleon justified a continuation of the war.

********

On the 7th June, 1800, the 82nd Regiment again embarked for foreign service, about seven hundred rank and file, under command of Lieutenant-Colonel Losack, and arrived at Quiberon Bay, where it joined the armament preparing to attack Belle Isle, and disembarked on the Isle of Houat on the 16th June. After some fruitless attempts were made, between the 16th and 22nd, to effect a landing on Belle Isle, the armament sailed for the Mediterranean, and, passing Gibraltar, learned the result of the Battle of Marengo. They then sailed for the Island of Minorca, and landed there on the 18th July.

This island had been occupied on the 15th November, 1798, by General the Hon. Charles Stewart and a British force, which had accompanied an expedition detached by Admiral the Earl St. Vincent early in the same month to take possession of Minorca, and thus enable the squadron to watch the French arsenals in the Mediterranean from a secure port.

The 82nd remained in the Island of Minorca till the peace of Amiens on the 3rd June, 1802, when Minorca being ceded to Spain, the 82nd was ordered home, and arrived at the Cove of Cork on the 28th July, but was detained twelve days in quarantine. It landed on the 9th August and proceeded to Newry, reaching that place after a march of fifteen days. It then mustered five hundred and eighty rank and file, having left one hundred and thirty men in hospital at Minorca.

It soon afterwards marched to Armagh, and in less than a

week afterwards to Omagh; and before the end of this year one hundred and eighty men were discharged, the greater part of whom had been enlisted to serve during the war only.

Recruiting was carried on during 1803.

In June, 1804, the regiment marched from Omagh to Mullingar, and thence, in July, to the Curragh of Kildare, where it formed part of the force collected in a camp of manoeuvre, under Lieutenant-General Lord Cathcart This camp broke up in the middle of September, when the Regiment returned to Mullingar.

By this time one hundred and fifty men had been recruited, and orders were received to form a second battalion again in England, to be composed of men raised under the Army of Reserve Act; and Lieutenant-Colonel Smith, from half-pay of the 20th Foot, was appointed to the command. This battalion was embodied at Horsham, and proceeded to Chichester in March of the following year.

Early in 1805 the first battalion marched to Dublin, where it remained, doing garrison duty, until the beginning of. August, when it was again encamped on the Curragh for the same purpose as last year. Thence it went to Limerick, and afterwards to Cork. In September it received a draft of two hundred and forty men from the second battalion, stationed since May at Littlehampton. These men were chiefly volunteers from the English militia.

In May, 1806, it received another draft of one hundred men from the second battalion, which had been stationed at Uxbridge since November of the previous year. These were volunteers for general service raised under the Army of Reserve Act.

In March, 1807, another draft of ninety men came from the second battalion, then quartered in Derby, to which place it had gone in November last year. These were volunteers of the same description as the last draft.

On the 5th July, 1807, the first battalion embarked at Cork, under command of Lieutenant-Colonel Smith, for the Downs. It disembarked at Deal, remained there a few days, and then marched to Ramsgate, where it re-embarked for Copenhagen, with the 32nd and 50th Regiments—forming Major-General Spencer's brigade of the army under Lord Cathcart, on the Island of Zeeland.

The following extracts from Sir Edward Cust's *Annals of the Wars* will explain the object of this expedition against Copenhagen. Nothing had hitherto been able to stay the triumphs of Napoleon, for he had fought his way from Montenotte to Friedland without a check. After three of the most decisive victories ever gained by one man within four months, Napoleon saw the European continent at his disposal.

> An expedition had been projected by the British Government to create a diversion in favour of Russia and Prussia before the decisive victory of Friedland had put an end to the campaign. Yet enough had transpired of the conferences at Tilsit to make it evident that having now scattered to the winds all the enemies who threatened his power on the continent, Napoleon was prepared to strain every nerve to make an impression on Great Britain. An imaginary statement of the French Emperor's designs at this period describes his plan to have been to embody the whole maritime forces of the continent against the British Navy. Of this immense naval power, the last division—consisting of fifteen sail of the line—reposed at this moment in the waters of Copenhagen. Under these circumstances a daring and vigorous resolution was adopted by the British Government, similar, though on a grander scale, to what had often been practised in war to deprive the enemy of the prize he thought to be actually in his grasp, and to convert to their own defence some of the resources on which he relied for his attack. And on the 19th July the Cabinet determined to get possession of the Danish fleet.
>
> On the 26th and 27th July an expedition set sail from Yarmouth Roads, counting ninety pendants, together with three hundred transports, having on board twenty thousand troops, under command of Major-General Sir Arthur Wellesley. The transports from the Island of Ru-

gen joined this expedition on the 3rd August, bringing the troops under Lieutenant-General Lord Cathcart, who was to command the land forces in chief, and which now consisted of twenty-seven thousand troops.

The entire armament cast anchor in appalling strength before the Island of Zeeland, which was surrounded and blockaded on every side.

On the morning of the 16th August, the troops were landed without resistance at Wedbeck, about twelve miles from the capital, towards which they commenced their march on the following day. Meanwhile the Danish militia were advancing along the Island of Zeeland, and Lord Cathcart directed Wellesley, with a division of four thousand men, to disperse them.

The 82nd formed the left of that part of the army which besieged the city of Copenhagen; and although the junior regiment, it occupied, by special order of the Major-General, the important post of the Windmill, on the extreme left, which it maintained during the whole of the operations. For its gallantry at this post it was specially praised in the public despatches of the Commander of the Forces, as well as in general orders. Lieutenant-Colonel Smith was subsequently knighted in consequence.

On the 1st September, Major-General Peymann was summoned, but he returned a direct negative. The British batteries opened on the 2nd September, and the town was set on fire by the first flight of Congreve rockets, which were here employed for the first time, and the citadel was given up to the British troops on the 8th. The loss of the British was fifty-six killed and two hundred wounded.

The last division of the British army re-embarked on the 20th, and returned to England. The artillery taken amounted to three thousand five hundred pieces.

The loss of the 82nd Regiment before Copenhagen was—Ensign Dixon and seven rank and file killed, Captain Hastings (lost an arm) and several men wounded.

Amongst the chargers brought over to England was a mare, which, after her safe return, produced a colt, named 'Copenhagen.' This horse, afterwards sold to Major-General Sir Charles Stewart, was taken by him to the Peninsula; and when that officer quitted the army, in 1813, it became the property of the Duke of Wellington. At Vittoria and other battles his Grace used no other charger, and it became a great favourite with him. This horse also carried the Duke throughout the glorious day of Waterloo, when, it is said, he bore him for eighteen hours on his back and gave no signs of fatigue. He was a full rich chestnut colour, with a strong dash of the Arab in his appearance. He died in 1835, at the age of twenty-seven years, and was buried at Strathfield Saye with military honours. 'Copenhagen' was modelled for the horse of the Wellington Statue upon the Arch in London.

During the absence of the first battalion on active service, the second battalion had successively moved to Hull, Burlington, and Scarborough.

Returning to England, the first battalion landed five companies at Deal on the 4th November, whence they marched to Portsmouth, whither the other five companies had proceeded by sea, there to form a force, composed of the 29th, 32nd, 50th, and 82nd, for secret service, under Major-General Spencer.

Drafts from the second battalion and Irish militia here joined the first battalion, raising its strength to nine hundred and eighty rank and file. The success of the affair against Copenhagen had upset Napoleon's design of embodying the whole maritime forces of the Continent against the British navy.

> No sooner therefore was he arrived in Paris than he began to turn his eyes towards the Peninsula. He had previously fomented an intrigue, calculated to embroil the Royal Family of Spain in such a manner as that he might be called upon to arbitrate between them.
>
> A treaty was soon afterwards concluded at Fontainebleau, by which French troops were to be admitted into Spain, to be maintained and subsisted by that state for the conquest of Portugal. He had already formed a camp at

Bayonne, of which he had given the command to General Junot, who was now ordered to cross the frontier, and direct his march upon Lisbon. At the same time he prepared a second army, under General Dupont, in the camp at Boulogne, to be ready to follow Junot when required.

The Prince Regent of Portugal was at first determined to yield to Napoleon's demands, and exclude the commerce of Great Britain from Portugal, and he actually did this, by proclamation, dated 20th October; but the British Consul demanded his passports in consequence, and a British squadron of nine sail of the line, under Rear-Admiral Sir Sydney Smith, sent from England on receipt of the Prince Regent's proclamation, came to an anchor in the Tagus on the 17th November, and the port was declared to be in a state of blockade. The Portuguese fleet, being in readiness to put to sea, received on board the whole of the Royal Family, with its most faithful counsellors and adherents, amounting to eighteen thousand persons, with property to the amount of many millions value, and sailed for Brazil, in South America.

Junot pushed forward with all haste, and entered Lisbon on the morning of the 29th November. The regency was at once formally dissolved, and the ancient flag of Portugal was hauled down and the tri-colour hoisted in its place. Junot's army had entered Spain with the full consent of that Government, for the avowed purpose of making a conquest of Portugal, but on the 22nd November, without any authority asked or given, Dupont, with a second large army, marched upon Madrid, and these two armies then seized upon the four most important frontier towns of Spain, *viz.*:—Figueras, Barcelona, St. Sebastian, and Pampeluna.

The simultaneous and unanimous decision to resist oppression now manifested by the Spanish nation, when Napoleon unmasked his designs upon their country, must ever remain an enduring monument of the solid qualities which belong to this grand old people.[1]

1. Cust's *Annals of the Wars.*

On the 18th December, 1807, the first battalion of the 82nd, in company with the 29th, 32nd, and 50th, under command of Major-General Spencer, before mentioned as having been assembled at Portsmouth for secret service, sailed for Cadiz, but the fleet was dispersed on the 26th by a heavy gale in the Bay of Biscay, and this caused a separation of the Regiment for six months. Some of the companies found their way to Gibraltar, from whence they were despatched to Sicily, troops being required there in anticipation of a rupture with the Porte; the British Admiralty having already directed a force to be despatched to the Dardanelles. Other companies returned to England, whence they again sailed and reached Gibraltar in 1808. It was not, however, till the latter end of May, that the whole regiment again met off Cadiz, where Major-General Spencer's force had been ordered to rendezvous. The wisdom of employing English troops and English revenues against the French Emperor was manifest, for Napoleon had declared, that so soon as the whole continent had been conquered he would invade England. To keep his armies employed in the Peninsula, and to prevent the entire conquest of the continent, was evidently the most certain method of averting an invasion of England. Sir Arthur Wellesley's first object, therefore, was to defend Portugal, which thus became an outwork of the British Islands.

Major-General Spencer's force, consisting of the four regiments above named, was at anchor in the offing of the Bay of Cadiz when the French fleet surrendered on the 10th May, 1808.

This division was landed at Puerto Santa Maria, opposite Cadiz, and after remaining there some time, embarked and sailed for Mondego Bay, midway between Oporto and Lisbon.

On the 1st August, the army under Lieutenant-General Sir Arthur Wellesley commenced landing at Mondego Bay, and as the last brigade disembarked, Major-General Spencer's division arrived most opportunely from Cadiz, and came to anchor the same evening. This reinforcement raised Wellesley's army to the effective strength of twelve thousand three hundred men.

The French general Junot had divided his force of forty-five thousand men, into three corps of infantry and one of cavalry. All the fortresses of the kingdom were at this time in his possession, and in perfect repair, garrisoned and provisioned. The news that a British army had landed in Mondego Bay reached Lisbon on the 2nd August. Junot marched at once to encounter the British with two divisions amounting to between thirteen and fourteen thousand men, and all the detachments he had with him in Lisbon.

On joining Sir Arthur Wellesley's force the 82nd Regiment was appointed to Brigadier-General Nightingall's brigade in Major-General Spencer's division.

Wellesley marched on the 8th August, and first met the French in a skirmish on the 15th on the road to Rolica. The French had taken up a good position and had resolved to await the assault. About 7 a.m. on the 17th, Sir Arthur marched against the enemy with fourteen thousand men, and eighteen guns, in three columns of attack—Hill's brigade on the right, and Ferguson's on the left. Wellesley himself commanded the centre, consisting of the brigades of Beresford, Fane, and Nightingall; in the latter of which was the 82nd. These brigades, with two batteries, moved along the high road against the enemy's front. The French made a retrograde movement and fell back to some rocky heights. The defence was desperate. The French general, Laborde, was wounded, and being unable to maintain his ground, gradually drew away his troops. The action of Rolica lasted from 9 a.m. till 5 p.m., and the French loss was three guns and six hundred men. The British loss did not exceed five hundred. The want of cavalry and the rocky nature of the ground, prevented this first success of the English army from being as complete as it might have been.

Junot quitted Lisbon on the 16th August, and came up with Laborde's retreating army at Torres Vedras, and was soon after joined by Loison.

Wellesley had not pursued Laborde, but marched close to the shore, to cover the landing of some reinforcements which had been sighted off the coast.

On the evening of the 19th he took up a position beside the village of Vimiera. Two brigades were landed from the transports, and joined him on the 20th, which increased his force to sixteen thousand men and eighteen guns. Thus reinforced, he resolved to advance upon Lisbon, and had projected a flank march to turn the French left.

On the night of the 20th Lieutenant-General Sir Harry Burrard arrived from England to supersede Sir Arthur in command, and forbade the march projected by the latter, because he expected Sir John Moore with reinforcements.

The French appeared, at 7 a.m. on the 21st, within four miles of the British outposts.

The position at Vimiera was a steep mountain ridge, resting on the sea, and tending towards a plateau, on which the village ofVimiera was situated.

Junot ordered the French cavalry to turn the English flank, while he sent three brigades to assail the plateau.

Wellesley reinforced his left by four brigades from the right before the attack commenced.

The position was broken and wooded, and the French could not be discerned before they burst upon the English centre, but they could not get through the British line.

Towards noon, Junot, seeing that he could not pierce the centre, sent forward two brigades to turn a ravine on the English left, from which they were driven back with a loss of six guns. They were then retiring from these attacks when they were charged by the British and Portuguese cavalry. The English reserve had not been yet brought forward; and when Sir Arthur was asked whether Anstruther's brigade should be brought up to his assistance, he replied, "No, Sir. I am not pressed, and I want no assistance. I am beating the French, and am able to beat them wherever I find them."

At two o'clock in the day Junot's retreat was an unquestionable fact, and Sir Arthur desired to follow up the -Victory and cut off his retreat upon Lisbon; but Sir Harry Burrard issued orders to the army to halt and pile arms, for the expected arrival of Sir John Moore. Sir Arthur, turning to his staff, said, "Gentlemen, nothing now remains to be done but to go and shoot red-legged partridges."

The British loss in these two actions of Rolica and Vimiera[2] was one thousand two hundred and twenty; that of the French, two thousand five hundred. The 82nd was particularly mentioned in the despatches sent to England by the commander of the forces, for its gallantry in the latter action. It lost on the two occasions, Lieutenant Donkin and fifteen rank and file killed, and Lieutenant Bead and several men wounded. Major Eyre commanded in both actions, and was immediately promoted to the Lieutenant-Colonelcy of the 19th foot. The French army had now been defeated in two successive battles, and the French generals agreed that they must have recourse to some species of negotiation. Hence the convention of Cintra which followed immediately afterwards.

********

Lieutenant-General Sir Hew Dalrymple had arrived from England, with authority to assume the supreme command. With surprise he received on the 22nd the French proposals for negotiations, and at once appointed Sir Arthur Wellesley and the Quartermaster-General, Lieutenant-Colonel Murray, to conduct the conference.

There was no hesitation in admitting an armistice for forty-eight hours. The succession of three different Generals to the chief command was not likely to be productive of much vigour. The British ultimatum, however, was that the French should quit Portugal, and that all the strong places should be restored to the Portuguese authorities: to which Junot gladly put his seal. But difficulties soon arose as to the meaning of preliminary terms, and the British General denounced the armistice on the 28th. In the meantime, Sir John Moore, with eleven thousand men, had disembarked at the mouth of the Tagus, and Junot, seeing himself outnumbered, conceded the points in dispute. The

2. Rolica and Vimiera are both borne on the regimental colour of the 82nd. Rolica is spelt incorrectly on the colour, Sir Arthur Wellesley's writing not being plain.

Convention of Cintra was then signed, and ratified on the 31st, under which the French set sail from Lisbon early in September, 1808, landed on the coast of Brittany, and at once marched to enter the Peninsula by way of the Pyrenees. The Russian Fleet of nine sail of the line and a frigate was held by his Britannic Majesty as a deposit until, six months after, a treaty of peace was signed between Russia and Great Britain. The officers and crews were to be sent to their own country, at England's expense. The indignation of the British nation at the Convention of Cintra was unbounded; but it was, notwithstanding, advantageous to England, under the circumstances. It delivered Portugal from the French, and gave possession of fortresses which would have cost much time and blood to take; and Lisbon became an excellent *place d'armes*, the possession of which by land and sea secured a base for future operations against the enemy.

Previous to the army being ordered into cantonments, thirteen officers and more than a third of the men of the 82nd went into hospital with fever, from having been encamped on marshy ground. This prevented the Regiment from marching with Sir John Moore into Spain. It was sent by sea to garrison Oporto, and, on removal from Nightingall's Brigade, the following order was issued:

> St Antonio de Fayal
> Camp
> 6th Sept., 1808
> B.O.
> Brigadier-General Nightingall cannot allow the 82nd Regiment to leave the 3rd Brigade without expressing his sincere regret at losing so distinguished a corps. Their soldier-like conduct during the whole time he has had the honour to command them, entitles them to every mark of his approbation and praise; but their brilliant conduct in the glorious victory of the 21st ultimo (Vimiero) has made impressions on his mind which can never be effaced. The Brigadier- General therefore requests that Major Eyre and the officers and soldiers of the 82nd Regiment will accept

his best thanks for their orderly and meritorious conduct during the above period, and to rest assured that he shall ever regret their being removed from his brigade.

The sea voyage and three months' rest in quarters so far improved the health of the corps, that it was reported by Lieutenant-General Mackenzie Frazer, who inspected it on the 25th December, 1808, to be fit for the field, and it was ordered to join the army in Spain, and proceeded to Benevente, where it was appointed to Brigadier-General Fane's brigade, in Mackenzie Frazer's division.

On the 16th January, 1809, the Regiment was present at the action of Corunna, but not actively engaged.

The excitement caused in England by the Convention of Cintra had rendered the presence of Sir Hew Dalrymple, Sir Henry Burrard, and Sir Arthur Wellesley necessary at home. Accordingly, the Command-in-Chief of the British Army in Portugal devolved on Lieutenant-General Sir John Moore.

Sir John so divided his army as to send the artillery with a column to advance by Badajoz and Talavera, while the rest should proceed to Almeida. Lieutenant-General the Hon. John Hope, Major-General Beresford, and Lieutenant-General Frazer proceeded by different routes to the same destination. Sir John Moore intended that all these separate divisions should unite at Salamanca with a corps under Sir David Baird, which had been landed at Corunna. The general himself left Lisbon on the 27th October, 1808, for Almeida, and on the 13th November he reached Salamanca, where he halted to assemble his army.

Napoleon had arrived at Bayonne on the 3rd November, and reached Vittoria, escorted by the cavalry of his guard, on the 5th November, where he established himself. He had brought with him out of France Marshal Soult, who took the command of a corps and moved on Burgos, where he soon overthrew the Spanish army under the Marquis de Belvidere. Napoleon then moved his headquarters to Burgos, where he arrived incognito on the 11th.

Sir John Moore heard of these events at Salamanca on the

13th, and two nights later he received intelligence that the enemy was at Valladolid within twenty leagues of his headquarters, while he had no reason to expect any effective co-operation from the Spanish armies which had now been annihilated.

Napoleon heard at Burgos of Moore's advance into Spain, and directed both Soult and Junot to proceed against him.

Sir John heard on the 28th of the dispersion of the Spanish armies. He had been deceived by the representations of the British ministers at Madrid and Lisbon, and at once resolved to withdraw his army altogether out of Spain, and assemble it on the banks of the Tagus. The British ministers wrote strongly to dissuade him from his determination. Overpowered by entreaties and persuasions, he altered his plans, and on the 21st December moved his whole army to Sahagun, and there established his headquarters.

Marshal Soult was considerably taken aback by this bold advance of Moore, and resolved to march against him on the 23rd. Moore counted on having twenty-three thousand infantry, two thousand three hundred cavalry, and sixty guns.

As soon as Napoleon heard of Moore's advance, he ordered Soult to retire before him to Burgos, to which city he likewise directed Junot to advance in all haste, while he himself resolved to quit Madrid on the 18th, and march against the English army in person. On the 24th, Moore became aware of the danger of his position and gave orders for an immediate retreat, satisfied with having withdrawn the emperor from the capital; on the 28th he reached Benevente. The weather was most inclement, and Napoleon, leading his army through the passes, was so overwhelmed by a snow storm, that a column of infantry actually retreated before it; but he, having recently made a glorious winter campaign in Poland, was not to be beaten by a snow storm in Spanish mountains. Immediately, riding to the front, he formed the chasseurs of the guard into subdivisions on foot the width of the road, who leading their horses, formed a shelter to those who followed. On the 29th December, he approached Benevente. The British cavalry destroyed the bridge leading into

Benevente, and had a successful cavalry affair near Villapando. Sir John Moore now ordered the destruction of all stores, and Lord Paget covered the retreat with the cavalry. On the morning of the 29th, between five hundred and six hundred cavalry of the Imperial Guard crossed the river by the fords of the Esla. The pickets, amounting to about two hundred and twenty men, under Lieutenant-Colonel Otway, Major of the 18th Hussars, showed a good face to the enemy. On the 30th, the British general reached Astorga, and continued his retreat next day on Villa Franca. On the 31st, Napoleon came up with his head quarters to Astorga, and then gave up the pursuit to Marshal Soult. He had received information that the Austrians were preparing to take the field, which obliged him to hasten back to Paris. The weather was dreadful; rain, snow, and mud, rendered the roads almost impassable. The British Commander-in-chief was constantly with his rearguard. A curious anecdote is related among the incidents of Moore's retreat, by the French General Savary, in his memoirs:

> We found many English cavalry horses dead in the road, and we observed that they all wanted one foot. We learned afterwards, that the English cavalry soldiers who lost their horses were each obliged to carry a foot to his captain to prove that his horse was dead, otherwise he would be suspected of having sold it.

On the 3rd January, 1809, while Sir John Moore was with the rearguard, five thousand French came sharply up, and as they now pressed the retreat, Moore ordered a halt at Lugo, where he determined to show a front and give battle to the enemy. Some skirmishing ensued until night came on, when the rearguard fell back on Lugo. Lugo is a walled town standing on an eminence and surrounded by cultivated enclosures, which offer good cover for marksmen and impede the action of cavalry.

The British halted here on the 6th January, and Soult reached San Juan de Corbo. On the 7th the French opened a cannonade, but postponed their attack till the 9th, as Laborde's division and other reinforcements were coming up. In the night of the 8th-9th the retreat was resumed. The troops, jaded and half-famished, got into complete disorganisation, and were little better than a confused crowd of stragglers. Much baggage was lost, and at one point treasure to the amount of £25,000 was sacrificed by throwing it over a precipice. On the 11th the army reached Corunna, without having left a gun or a colour in possession of the enemy. On nearing Corunna, Sir John saw with alarm that the transports had not arrived, and he had now nothing left but to accept battle in the best position he could select, to check the French, who came up on the morning of the 12th. The 13th passed in making dispositions on both sides, and the French constructed a battery of twelve guns, which enfiladed the whole British line from right to centre. On a hill a little removed from the town of Corunna a magazine of about four thousand barrels of gunpowder remained, which had been brought from England and deposited there for the Spaniards. Having removed as many barrels as were required, the rest were blown up, with an explosion that shook the ground like an earthquake, to the astonishment of both armies. On the 14th the enemy commenced a cannonade, which was returned by the British Artillery, and he drew off his guns. In the evening of the same day the fleet of transports hove in sight, and preparations were forthwith made for the embarkation of the army. Many thousands of the cavalry horses were necessarily shot on the strand, in order that they might not become a prize to the enemy. Moore prepared for an offensive movement as soon as the time should arrive. About noon of the 16th he was on the ground. At 2 p.m. the enemy opened fire, and the whole French line advanced at once, preceded by clouds of skirmishers. The 4th, 50th, and 42nd defended the right, while the old 95th Rifles were extended amongst the underwood, to check the French skirmishers, whose heavy guns swept the British line with round shot, grape, and canister. The French left having carried the village of Elvina, divided into two parts, one attacking the front, the other the right of Baird's Division, while their right advanced upon Palacio against Hope. The 50th Regiment forced the French back, with great loss, quite beyond the houses of Elvina. The enemy being reinforced, renewed the fight beyond the village, and Elvina became the scene of another contest, when Moore himself charged at the head of the 42nd Highlanders. Later in the day he was struck by a cannon ball in the left shoulder. Paget's division drove back the French, but the approach of night prevented any further advance; and Hope's division assailed and regained possession of the village of Palacio. Thus ended the Battle of Corunna—

> . . . .which not only gave a glorious termination to a disastrous retreat, but afforded an imperishable proof of the pluck of British soldiers under the most trying and adverse circumstances

They not only repulsed Soult's attack, but carried forward their line considerably beyond the ground occupied before the action. Hope ordered the troops to quit the field by brigades, as if marching home from a field-day; and they passed through the town to the place of embarkation. The entire army was put on board the ships during the night. The rearguard remained on shore till noon on the 17th, when it embarked without being molested, and the French fired a few harmless shots at the transports as they got under weigh. Some of the ships, however, were afterwards in confusion, cut their cables and ran ashore, where they were set fire to, and the soldiers shifted to other vessels; which was effected without a single casualty.

At twelve o'clock on the night of the battle, the remains of Sir John Moore were removed to the citadel of Corunna; he was merely wrapped in his military cloak and blankets, and buried on the ramparts by a party of the 9th Regiment by torchlight and in silence.

In consequence of fever and the casualties which occurred during this retreat and battle, the 82nd, when it landed at Portsmouth on the 8th February, 1809, did not muster more than two-thirds of the number which had marched out of Oporto. On disembarking, it proceeded to Lewes, in Sussex, and, during April and May, the first battalion received two hundred men from different militia regiments, as well as a draft of two hundred and fifty men from the second battalion now quartered at

Scarborough, so that five months after its return from Spain it consisted of one thousand one hundred rank and file, and was ordered to form part of the army assembled at Portsmouth under Lieutenant-General the Earl of Chatham for the Walcheren expedition. It embarked in command of Lieutenant-Colonel Grant on the 16th July, and was posted to Major-General Houston's brigade.

About the middle of May, 1809, the Austrian Ambassador at the Court of St James urged the departure of this expedition for the Scheldt. Thirty thousand infantry and eight thousand cavalry were the disposable force. On the 10th June all the troops were ready, but discussions as to the choice of a commander-in-chief delayed their departure. The Earl of Chatham was finally nominated to the command, and Admiral Sir Richard Strachan led the naval squadron. The fleet having first assembled in the Downs, steered for the mouths of the Scheldt. The object of this expedition was to destroy Antwerp, its dockyards, and shipping.

Since the year 1792 the conquest of Belgium had always been a cause of uneasiness. The Scheldt being connected with the interior by a canal, through which timber and other materials could be conveyed all over the world, France would derive every advantage in possessing that river, should she ever make a descent on the coast of England. The political state of Holland was a subordinate question. This English expedition was signalled on the morning of the 29th July, 1809, and anchored to the north of Cadzand and Walcheren. The 82nd Regiment landed at Walcheren on the 2nd August. On the 30th the invasion of the last-named island was effected. On the third day after disembarking the English army found itself four leagues in a direct line from Antwerp, and could have reached it in a few hours, for at low water the entrance of the eastern Scheldt or Canal of Bergen-op-Zoom forms a wide ford. Here the Earl of Chatham halted and employed his army to besiege Flushing—a place which would necessarily fall after the taking of Antwerp, and which was useless to him at present. Had he advanced rapidly upon Antwerp he would have found the forts and the defences of the Scheldt unprepared. Napoleon had been deceived as to the destination of these armaments. He believed they were intended for Spain. There is no doubt that at this time the English could have destroyed the French squadron and burned the dockyards. Antwerp and the frontier places only contained weak depots of the regiments engaged outside. There was no other army. This delay saved Antwerp, for the French saw their mistake and quickly profited by it. The talent displayed here by the Chef de Bataillon Bernard so pleased the Emperor that he placed him on his personal staff. The French Admiral immediately collected his squadron—one part of which was cruising before Flushing and the other part stationed beyond Bate—and brought them under the walls of the fortress. On the first appearance of the English army the French generals marched on Antwerp and on Cadzand, and were very soon in position to meet the English, should they attempt to force the passage of the Scheldt or attack Antwerp. In a few hours these proceedings were telegraphed to Paris, and orders rapidly returned by the same means. On the 2nd August the French War Minister announced to Napoleon that twenty thousand men, under Rampon, were moving upon Antwerp, where they arrived on the 6th August. The defence of the place itself, and the forts surrounding it, were soon completed, and by the 8th, both the city and the fleet were secure. By the 14th they had fifty-two thousand men collected in and around Antwerp.

The Earl of Chatham had assembled the greater part of his force to besiege Flushing, while the remaining portion were still on board ship. On the 11th August, ten frigates forced the entrance to the Western Scheldt, and on the 13th, about half past eleven, the land batteries commenced their fire from thirty mortars and ten heavy guns, and Congreve rockets were thrown into the town. At mid-day on the 14th, eight ships and four frigates opened fire on the works, and conflagrations were observed in the interior. On the 15th, at two a.m., the place capitulated, and four thousand men laid down their arms and were taken prisoners to England.

On the investment of Flushing, the brigade of Major-General Houston was ordered to advance left in front, when the 82nd Regiment led, and was engaged on the great road from the moment it passed Middlebourg till within half gunshot of the fortress, and obliged the enemy to leave in their possession two guns and some baggage. Lieutenants Pratt and Bead and a few men of the 82nd were wounded on this occasion.

Lord Chatham had more than thirty thousand soldiers and sailors ill or dead. The corps before Flushing suffered fearfully from the terrible fever of the country, which daily spread amongst them with frightful rapidity. More than half the army were in hospital. Napoleon thus wrote:

> I am glad to see the English congregate in the swamps of Zeeland. If we can only keep them there, the bad climate and the peculiar fever of the country will soon destroy their army.

In September, the first division of the army, in which was the 82nd, returned to England, and the regiment was at once sent to its old quarters at Lewes.

********

The Peninsular campaigns had commenced with Rolica and Vimiera, in 1808; but it was not until Sir Arthur Wellesley's second appearance in Portugal, the following year, that the real struggle took place, and the three great decisive battles of the war were fought—Talavera, Salamanca, and Vittoria. At Talavera the power of Napoleon in the Spanish Peninsula was checked, at Salamanca it was destroyed, and at Vittoria he and his armies were thrust out of Spain.

On the 12th May, 1809, Sir Arthur crossed the Douro, at Oporto, in the face of the French army, and drove them out of Portugal. On the 27th June, at the head of twenty-two thousand British troops and thirty guns, he entered Spain and advanced towards Madrid. A Spanish army, under Cuesta, of thirty thousand men, was to co-operate. Great delay was occasioned by the want of supplies. In Sir Arthur's despatch to Lord Castlereagh at this period, he writes:

> I am not able to follow the enemy as I could wish, having found it impossible to procure even one mule or a cart in Spain. My troops have been in actual want of provisions for the last two days. The French can take what they like, and will take it, while we cannot even buy common necessaries.

Marshals Jourdan and Victor, with fifty-six thousand French veterans, marched to meet the English army at Talavera. On the 27th July, Sir Arthur narrowly escaped being taken prisoner in an affair of outposts; ten thousand Spaniards broke and fled, but the French were beaten off. They then made an attack on the key of the English position, and succeeded for a moment, until reinforcements arrived and drove them back. In this affair the English lost eight hundred men, and the French one thousand. It was long after dark when the attack was finally repulsed, and at daylight on the 28th it was renewed. There was hand-to-hand fighting. Major-General Rowland Hill was wounded. But after a severe contest the French withdrew.

The position now occupied by the British had the city of Talavera and the Tagus on the right; a circular hill, strengthened by earthworks, on the left; and a ravine and watercourse in front. The hill was the key of the position, and as Sir Arthur discovered two French columns advancing to it, he ordered cavalry to charge. The late 23rd Light Dragoons and a regiment of German Hussars were despatched on this duty. A chasm in the ground stopped the Germans, while many of the English leaped it, and thus broken fell upon the French infantry; but they were immediately charged by some Polish Lancers, and lost two hundred officers and men. The French obstinately contended for the hill, while a strong body of their infantry crossed the watercourse in front, and attempted to break the English centre. This attack failed, and the Guards impetuously followed the enemy beyond their lines, where they were in turn charged by the French reserves, and for a moment the English centre was in danger. But Sir Arthur seeing the Guards start in pursuit, and suspecting the consequence, at once brought up the 48th Regiment, which checked the enemy until the Guards could reform, when the French were driven over the ravine, their general mortally wounded, and the battle was won. Night closed upon both armies in their original positions; but at daylight next morning the French commenced a retreat. The English loss was about five thousand, and included two generals killed and three wounded. The French lost seven thousand killed and wounded, besides seventeen guns. General Jomini says:

> This battle finally established the fame of Marlborough's descendants, which had declined during the last century. It was now acknowledged that the British infantry could hold their own against the best in Europe.[4]

At the end of the battle, the long dry grass with which the field was covered accidentally took fire.

> Some hundreds of wounded men, unable to crawl out of reach of the flames, were thus burnt to death.

The 82nd was represented in this battle by one major, one captain, four sergeants, and sixty rank and file, who had been left sick in Portugal They formed part of the first battalion of detachments, and lost five rank and file killed and wounded. Sir Arthur was immediately created Baron Douro and Viscount Wellington of Talavera. He had only nineteen thousand English and Germans and thirty thousand useless Spaniards, against fifty thousand French veterans, under two of Napoleon's ablest generals.

In 1810 Napoleon determined to conquer the whole Peninsula, and he increased his armies to three hundred and sixty-six thousand men, of whom eighty-six thousand, under Massena, were intended for the conquest of Portugal.

When the 82nd returned to England with the first division of the army, after Walcheren, it was sent to its old quarters—Lewes, in Sussex—about the middle of September, 1809, where it had scarcely been a month before it was ordered to re-embark every man fit for duty to Flushing; and consequently, two hundred rank and file, under Major King, proceeded a second time to Walcheren, where they remained until that island was finally evacuated.

4. Cust's *Wars*.

In December, 1809, the second battalion marched from Scarborough to Hull

In February, 1810, although the first battalion was still suffering from the effects of the Walcheren fever, and was in a state little better than convalescent, it received orders to embark for Gibraltar, where it arrived on the 31st March. In April, 1810, the second battalion moved from Hull to Tynemouth.

On the 13th October, 1810, the first battalion embarked in the Spanish hulk *El Vincendas*, to join an expedition against Malaga, under command of Major-General Lord Blayney; and on the 15th, when off Cape Frangerola, H.M.S. *Topaz* signalled from in-shore that Lord Blaney "had landed on the 14th, and was in want of immediate assistance." Seven boats from H.M.S. *Rodney*, were sent to the hulk, and conveyed to the shore about eighty rank and file of the flank companies of the 82nd, with Lieutenant-Colonel Grant. On their landing it was found that Lord Blaney and the guns had fallen into the hands of the enemy, and that the army had retreated to the shore. Lieutenant-Colonel Grant—being unable to rally the retreating troops—took up a position which kept the enemy in check until about four p.m., when the embarkation was effected. The remainder of the battalion, being at least twelve miles from the shore, could not be landed for want of boats.

On this occasion Lieutenant Bead was wounded.

On the return of the battalion to Gibraltar the Lieutenant-General addressed the following to Lieutenant-Colonel Grant:

> Gibraltar
> October, 1810
> Had it not been for the steadiness of the few of the 82nd under your orders, together with the able assistance of H. M. S. Rodney who covered the retreat, the embarkation could not have been effected; for which I beg you to accept my warmest acknowledgments.
> *Colin Campbell*
> Lieutenant-General

The flank companies of the 82nd formed a part of Lieutenant Colonel Brown's flank battalion at the battle of Barrosa, and received their full share of Lieutenant-General Graham's praise for their conduct in this action, where they suffered considerably, having had five rank and file killed, and Captain Stewart, Lieutenant McKay, two sergeants, and eighty men wounded.

Towards the close of February, 1811, an expedition was organized to attack the rear of the French army under Marshal Victor, blockading Cadiz. Seven thousand Spanish troops, under General La Pena, and a British force of three thousand under Lieutenant-General Graham, afterwards Lord Lynedoch, were embarked at Cadiz and disembarked at Algeciras. They then marched to Tarifa, and moved thence on the 28th. On the 5th March the allied army, after marching sixteen hours, arrived on the low ridge of Barrosa, four miles south of the Santi Petri River. The Spaniards were to attack the rear and left flank of the enemy's lines, while Graham was ordered to a position half way between Barrosa and the Santi Petri River. Expecting that the Spanish General would have left a division to defend the hill, the baggage of the English army remained there under a guard composed of the flank companies of the 9th and 82nd Regiments, in command of Lieutenant-Colonel Brown, 28th Foot; and Graham's astonishment was extreme, when he discovered that the hill was almost unoccupied. The French Marshal saw the mistake also, and sent the whole of his disposable force, *viz.*, two divisions and five hundred horse, to seize the heights. A retreat would have endangered the whole of the allied army, and an immediate attack was determined on. The right wing of the English, in which were now the 82nd flank companies, proceeded to charge Rufin's division on the hill, and were successful. The contest was sanguinary, but the undaunted perseverance of the brigade of Guards and of Lieutenant-Colonel Brown's battalion, as well as of other detachments, overcame the French, and soon drove them down the hill in confusion, leaving two guns behind them. In less than an hour and a half the enemy was in full retreat, leaving an eagle, six guns, two wounded generals, and many killed and wounded on the field. The French numbered eight thousand, and their loss was three thousand. The allies lost one thousand two hundred and forty-three killed and wounded. Though the battle of Barrosa was amongst the minor actions, and had no important consequences, inasmuch as the blockade of Cadiz was not interrupted, yet in no instance during the war was British valour more conspicuous. Lieutenant-General Graham's despatch thus alludes to the gallantry of that portion of the force in which the 82nd was brigaded:

> The enemy, confident of success, met General Dilkes on the ascent of the hill, and the contest was sanguinary; but the undaunted perseverance of the brigade of Guards, and of Lieutenant-Colonel Brown's battalion, and of Lieutenant-Colonel Norcott's and Major Acheson's detachments, overcame every obstacle, and General Rufin's division was driven from the heights in confusion, leaving two pieces of cannon. No expressions of mine could do justice to the conduct of the troops throughout. Nothing less than the almost unparalleled exertions of every officer, the invincible bravery of every soldier, and the most determined devotion to the honour of His Majesty's arms in all, could have achieved this brilliant success, against such a formidable enemy so posted.

The brigade of Guards, the 28th Regiment, to which Lieutenant-Colonel Brown belonged, the 67th and 87th, and the Rifle Brigade, have all the word "Barrosa" on their colours and appointments; but the 82nd, and other corps merely represented by detachments, have not received the distinction, though the flank companies of the 25th and 40th Regiments have gained the word "Egypt," and those of the 61st the word "Peninsula," and nothing can be stronger than the General's expression of his satisfaction at the conduct of the various detachments engaged in this battle.

In September, 1811, the first battalion was increased by drafts from the second battalion, now stationed in Guernsey, to which island it had moved in June from Tynemouth. The strength of the first battalion on the 24th September, 1811, was forty-one officers, fifty-nine sergeants, twenty-one drummers, and one thousand one hundred and fifty rank and file.

Four companies formed part of the garrison of Tarifa during the siege of that place. Tarifa was an ancient town in the Straits of Gibraltar. It was surrounded by an old wall, without ditch or outworks, and its situation completely checked the coast traffic, by which the French army besieging Cadiz might obtain supplies, and the British general ordered it to be occupied by a small English garrison. Marshal Soult determined to take it from the allies, and directed Victor to drive the English out. Victor at once invested Tarifa with ten thousand men, and a breach was made in the old wall. Colonel Skerrett, who was in command, reported that on the evening of the 31st December, 1811, a strong French column was seen rapidly advancing to the breach, and preparations were forthwith made to receive them. In less than an hour victory was declared for the defenders, and the French column made a precipitate retreat. From that time the enemy kept up a partial fire, which widened the breach, and on the morning of January 5th, 1812, he was again seen advancing to the attack.

Colonel Skerrett wrote thus:

> The utmost effort of the French has been frustrated by one thousand eight hundred British and Spanish troops, with only the defence of a paltry wall; and an army of ten thousand men, conducted by a marshal of France, retreated from them silently in the night, after having been repulsed and defeated, leaving behind all their artillery and stores, collected at great expense and by immense exertions.

On the 9th June, 1812, the first battalion embarked at Gibraltar for Portugal, when Lieutenant-General Colin Campbell issued the following order:

> The first battalion of the 82nd Regiment will embark this day and proceed on its voyage to Lisbon.
>
> The Lieutenant-General feels great regret at parting with a corps which has on all occasions distinguished it-

self, as well in the field as in garrison. The memorable battle of Barrosa, and the gallant defence of Tarifa, bear ample testimony to the bravery and spirit possessed by this fine corps, and which is equally distinguished for its discipline. His Excellency will not fail to mark his approbation in the strongest manner to General the Earl of Wellington, under whose command the first battalion of the 82nd Regiment is destined to serve

After a protracted passage the regiment landed at Lisbon, and marched immediately to join the army at Cuellar, in Spain, nearly five hundred miles, where it arrived on the 5th August, and was posted to the fourth division, with which it continued until the end of the year, when the army retired into winter quarters.

In August of this year the Marquis of Wellington had reached Madrid after defeating the French at Salamanca, and he then undertook the siege of Burgos with the main body of his army. But Napoleon having suddenly concentrated his two armies, under Marshals Soult and Suchet, to raise the siege and to attack the troops in position on the Tagus, thus menacing the communications of the British army, the Allies were forced to abandon Madrid, quit the vicinity of Burgos, and retire towards Ciudad Rodrigo. From the want of food and the inclemency of the weather the troops suffered extremely; and on reaching the frontiers of Portugal, in November, the 82nd were sent to winter quarters, suffering from fever and diarrhoea to such an extent that nearly half the regiment was in hospital. This susceptibility to disease had probably its origin in the Walcheren expedition, and the fever which long continued to hang about the corps—six hundred cases of this malady having occurred while stationed at Gibraltar. During this winter the 82nd were in the cantonment of Santa Marinha, and lost two hundred and thirty men.

On the 29th December, a draft of five sergeants and ninety-seven rank and file joined from the second battalion, now stationed at Alderney, to which island it had moved in the month of May.

At the opening of the year 1813, the English had, including the Indian army and the militia at home and some foreign troops in her pay, a grand total of nine hundred and forty-nine thousand men under arms. The Marquis of Wellington had withdrawn for the winter to northern Portugal, while the French occupied central and eastern Spain.

In the month of May, 1813, Wellington's nominal force was two hundred thousand men, though only about half this number were fit to take the field. His principal army, composed of English and Portuguese, mustered about seventy-five thousand, of whom forty-four thousand were English.

On the 22nd May, 1813, he began his march, and crossed the stream which divides Portugal from Spain, exclaiming "Goodbye to Portugal."

The French, occupying the centre of Spain and defending the capital, were ready to fight; but Wellington, by continually threatening to turn their right flank and thus seize upon their communications, forced them back from Madrid to Burgos, and from Burgos to Vittoria, where King Joseph Bonaparte determined to fight for his kingdom; and into this place was poured all the artillery and baggage and stores, the king's valuables, the archives and papers of state, and a large amount of treasure, which had been in Madrid, Valladolid, and Burgos, and belonged to several different armies.

Vittoria is only twenty-six miles from Irun, on the French frontier. About the 15th June, 1813, King Joseph found his army, reckoning from sixty thousand to seventy thousand men, assembled round Vittoria. Wellington, haying left his sixth division behind, had now with him sixty thousand English and Portuguese, besides some Spanish troops. On the 21st June, the allied army attacked the enemy's position in front of Vittoria, which was approached by various mountain passes leading into the "basin of Vittoria," through which runs the river Zadora. The heights of Puebla formed the enemy's left, extending thence across the valley of Zadora. His centre occupied a height also commanding the valley, and his right was posted in Vittoria itself and on the passages of the river in its neighbourhood. Graham, with twenty thousand men, formed the left of the Allies; Hill, with an equal force, formed the right; and Wellington in person took the centre, intending to cross the Zadora and march direct upon Vittoria.

The 82nd was now in the first brigade of the seventh, or Lord Dalhousie's, division, belonging to Hill's corps, on the right; and for its conduct in this splendid victory was one of those particularly mentioned by the Marquis of Wellington in these terms:

> Major-General the Honourable Sir Charles Colville's brigade of the third division was seriously attacked on its advance by a very superior force, well formed, which it drove in, supported by Major-General Inglis's brigade of the seventh division, commanded by Colonel Grant of the 82nd. These officers, and the troops under their command, distinguished themselves.

Major King commanded the regiment while Colonel Grant commanded the brigade, and they both received a gold medal commemorative of the victory. The total loss of the British at Vittoria was one lieutenant-colonel, six captains, ten lieutenants, four ensigns, one staff, fifteen sergeants, four drummers, four hundred and sixty rank and file, and ninety-two horses, killed. One general-staff, seven lieutenant-colonels, five majors, forty captains, eighty-seven lieutenants, twenty-two ensigns, five staff, one hundred and twenty-three sergeants, thirteen drummers, two thousand five hundred and four rank and file, and sixty-eight horses, wounded. The loss of the 82nd was Lieutenant Carroll and five rank and file killed. Lieutenant-Colonel Grant, Lieutenants Davies, Derinzy, and Agnew, two sergeants, and thirty-four rank and file, wounded, and the regiment bears "Vittoria" on its colour and appointments.

For this victory, which drove the king and his army, in twenty-four hours, out of Spain, losing all their baggage, equipages and stores, artillery, treasure and papers, "so that no man could prove even how much pay was due to him," Lord Wellington was made a field-marshal. Having received Marshal Jourdan's baton, he sent it to the Prince Regent, who quickly returned him an English one in exchange. The allies lost upwards of five thousand men. The French loss in men was never ascertained, but they left—

> . . . . one hundred and fifty-one pieces of artillery, four hundred and fifteen wagons of ammunition, all their baggage, provisions, cattle, treasure, &c, and a considerable number of prisoners.[5]

The soldiers of the army got amongst them about a million sterling in money, besides rich vestures, gold and silver plate, pictures and jewels.

********

The 82nd was subsequently engaged in all the operations in the Pyrenees from the 25th July to 31st August, 1813, and for its gallantry on these occasions had the good fortune to be again particularly noticed by the Commander of the forces.

The French armies vanquished at Vittoria had retreated towards the Pyrenees by the Pampeluna Road, and the British at once followed in pursuit. Wellington's design was to invade France, and this could not be prudently undertaken without the previous capture of San Sebastian and Pampeluna. The former was therefore besieged and the latter blockaded. The allied armies were posted in the passes of the mountains to cover these two sieges. The seventh division, in which was the 82nd, occupied the heights of Santa Barbara, the town of Vera, and the Puerto de Echellar, and kept open the communication with the valley of Baztan, occupied by two divisions under Lieutenant-General Sir Rowland Hill. The English army, numbering eighty-two thousand men, extended from the mouth of the Bidassoa River on the left, to Roncesvalles, the crest of the principal chain of mountains on the right. The French army, under Marshal Soult, numbered seventy-seven thousand five hundred men. Their right was on the mountains overlooking the town of Vera, from the side of France, their left was at St. Jean Pied de Port, and their centre was on the heights between these two

5. Wellington's Despatches.

extremities, while their reserve guarded the Bidassoa from its mouth to Irun. The extent of the position varied from forty to sixty miles. The fortresses of Bayonne, St. Jean Pied de Port, San Sebastian, and Pampeluna, were all in possession of the French. The mountains were intersected by rocky precipices and passes, torrents and dense forests, forming, apparently, a wilderness where regular warfare would be impossible. The principal range of the Pyrenees separated Pampeluna on the Spanish side from San Sebastian and the other two fortresses on the French side. So that the English forces besieging Pampeluna and San Sebastian were cut off from one another. Wellington's occupation of the mountains supported both the besieging armies, and he was obliged to remain on the defensive until the enemy should make a decided attack on one or other of his flanks.

Soult's plan was to operate from St Jean Pied de Port and attack the allied right, and so force his way to relieve Pampeluna, but he formed two bridges over the Bidassoa near Irun, on the other flank, to induce a belief that he meant to relieve San Sebastian. On the 25th July, two divisions of the enemy's centre attacked Hill's position in the Puerto de Maya, at the head of the valley of Baztan. The 82nd being part of the force holding these heights, was under the immediate orders of Lieutenant-General Stewart, commanding the second division. Major William Fitzgerald, of the 82nd, was detached with a small force, composed of a part of his own regiment and a part of the gallant 71st, to occupy and hold a rocky ridge over Atchiola which commanded the approach on that side.

Count d'Erlon advanced to the attack with thirteen thousand men, and the intrepidity with which his assault was met, and the bravery with which every inch of ground was disputed, called forth the following gratifying notice from the lieutenant-general:

> I cannot too warmly praise the conduct of Major Fitzgerald, and that of his brave detachment. They maintained the position to the last, and were compelled from the want of ammunition to impede the enemy's occupation of the rock by hurling stones at them. I feel it my duty to recom-

mend to your attention and favourable report to the Commander of the forces, the conduct and spirit of Colonel Grant and of his brave corps, the 82nd Regiment; also the whole of the first brigade (composed of the 50th, 71st, and 92nd), than which his Majesty's army possesses not men of more approved discipline and courage. The wounds of him and every commanding officer in that brigade were attended with circumstances of peculiar honour to each of them, and to those under their orders.

The struggle was desperate, but by the opportune arrival of a brigade of the seventh division from Echellar under Major-General Barnes, the British troops still held their ground at nightfall The 82nd properly belonged to Inglis's brigade, in which were also the 51st and 68th, but when General Stewart reached the field of battle—

> . . . . he called down the 82nd from the mountain top and sent for aid to the seventh division. He was wounded but fought stoutly, for he was a gallant man. He was just going to abandon the mountain, when a brigade of the seventh division, led by General Barnes, arrived from Echellar, and charging, drove the French back to the Col de Maya.[6]

The Marquis of Wellington's despatch to Earl Bathurst, thus describes the affair:

> San Estevan
> August 1st, 1813
> Notwithstanding the enemy's superiority of numbers, they acquired but little advantage over these brave troops, during the seven hours they were engaged. All the regiments charged with the bayonet; the conduct of the 82nd Regiment, which moved up with Major-General Barnes's Brigade (consisting of the50th, 71st, and 92nd) is particularly reported. It is impossible that I can extol too highly the conduct of Major-General Barnes and these brave troops, which was the admiration of all who were witnesses of it.

6. Napier's *Peninsular War.*

The loss of the 82nd in this combat of Maya was one sergeant and seven rank and file killed; Colonel Grant, Captains Firman and Marshall, Ensign Lacy, seven sergeants, and sixty rank and file, wounded.

On the 27th July a battle was fought, in which the seventh division was not engaged.

> On the 29th the armies rested in position without firing a shot; but the wandering divisions on both sides were now entering the line.[7]

Marshal Soult, being unable to remain at such a distance from his supplies, resolved to place himself closer to his reserves, by which movement he expected to relieve San Sebastian entirely, the more so, as he thought his recent operations had detached from the force besieging that fortress a considerable number of troops. He therefore ordered his divisions to withdraw secretly from their left, and concentrate on their right upon Lizasso early on the morning of the 30th. In the night he had heard from deserters that Lizasso was to be attacked by three British divisions on the 30th.

> The same soldiers, on both sides, who had so strenuously combated at Maya on the 25th were again opposed in fight.[8]

On the night of the 29th and 30th the French had occupied in strength the crest of the mountain on the British left of the valley of the Lanz, and Lord Wellington determined to attack the position.

The seventh division swept over the hills beyond the Lanz River upon the right.

Hill was so posted behind Lizasso with ten thousand men as to cover the two roads leading from that place to the main road of communication between San Sebastian and Pampeluna.

Byng's brigade and the sixth division were combined to assault the village of Sauroren. These movements began at day-

---

7. Napier's *Peninsular War.*

8. Napier's *Peninsular War.*

light. Major-General Inglis, with only five hundred men of the seventh division, broke two French regiments, and drove them into the valley. The French division opposed to him was amazed and disordered by this sudden fall of five hundred men from the top of the mountain into their midst The village and bridge of Sauroren were covered with smoke, and tumult filled the valley, and the French divisions were entirely broken. The allies lost 1,900 men; on the French side the loss was enormous.

Wellington had ordered the Earl of Dalhousie, commanding the 7th division, to possess himself of the top of the mountain in his front, by which the enemy's right would be turned: and the spirited attack made by Inglis's brigade was the consequence. The 82nd took a prominent part in this attack, and obliged the enemy to abandon a position described by his Lordship as "one of the strongest and most difficult of access that he had yet seen occupied by troops." The loss of the 82nd in this battle was nine rank and file killed; Colonel Grant, Major Fitz Gerald, Lieutenants Mackay, Boyde, Wood, and Mason (all severely), and Lieutenant and Adjutant Holdsworth (slightly) wounded; ten sergeants and sixty-nine rank and file wounded.

With regard to this action, Napier writes thus:

> Yet neither Picton's advance, nor Cole's joint attack, nor Byng's assault on Sauroren, would have seriously damaged the French, without the sudden and complete success of Inglis beyond the Lanz. The key of the defence was in the ridge beyond the Lanz; and instead of two regiments, Clausel should have placed two divisions there.

Wellington drove the French before him beyond the Pass of Echellar, and finally fought two more battles, on the 1st and 2nd August. The two armies then rested quiet in their respective positions, after nine days of continued movement and ten serious actions. The Allies had lost seven thousand three hundred officers and soldiers killed and wounded or prisoners. Wellington now occupied his old positions from the pass of Roncesvalles to the mouth of the Bidassoa, and having little to fear from a renewed attack on Pampeluna, was wholly bent on the siege of San Sebastian.

While the siege was going on there was every reason to believe that the French would make an attempt to Aug. 31st, relieve the fortress, and Inglis's brigade, in which was the 82nd, moved up on the 30th August to attack the enemy at the camp of Urogue, on the opposite side of the Bidassoa, where the greater part of his force had been drawn together. Marshal Soult designed to fight a battle with the covering force at daybreak on the 30th, but his preparations being incomplete he deferred it until the 31st; and, to gain possession of the high road to St. Sebastian, he must of necessity win the heights of San Martial, now occupied by six thousand Spaniards.

A Portuguese brigade was posted on the heights ofVera and the slopes of the mountain.The British brigades were stationed higher up, under the convent of St Antonio, where they commanded the intersection of the roads leading from Vera and Lesaca.

Before daylight on the morning of the 31st the enemy crossed the Bidassoa by fords with a very large force, with which he made a most desperate attack along the whole front on the heights of San Martial, and the Spanish troops drove him back in most gallant style.

About the same time he also crossed the river in another place by fords below Salin, with three divisions of infantry, and attacked the Portuguese brigade there stationed.

Major-General Inglis's brigade was ordered up to support the Portuguese, and the Earl of Dalhousie supported Inglis with the whole of the seventh division. It was found impossible to maintain the heights between Lesaca and the Bidassoa, and they withdrew to those in front of the convent of St. Antonio, which was maintained. In this movement they were covered by the 51st and 68th Regiments. The enemy, unable to force the position, and finding his situation on the left becoming critical, retired during the night.

In these operations, by which the enemy attempted a second time to prevent the establishment of the Allies upon the frontiers of France, he was defeated.

The loss of the 82nd in killed and wounded in this action

was—Lieutenant Wilstead and four rank and file killed, Lieutenant Donellan and five sergeants and fifty-four rank and file wounded. Inglis lost two hundred and seventy men and twenty-two officers out of his brigade alone.

The total loss sustained by the regiment in the three days' fighting was—one lieutenant-colonel, one major, two captains, eight subalterns, twenty-three sergeants, and two hundred and four rank and file, including killed and wounded.

Colonel Grant was decorated with a clasp for these actions, and the regiment bears on its colours and appointments "Pyrenees."

A detachment of ten sergeants and two hundred rank and file joined from the second battalion, twenty-four hours previous to the last action, in which they were engaged and showed uncommon spirit. Sebastian After a siege extending over sixty-three days of open trenches, and after three furious assaults, the fortress and town of St Sebastian fell on the 8th September, and the Spanish flag was hoisted under a salute of twenty-one guns. Napier says:

> A thunder-storm coming down from the mountains immediately after the place was carried added to the confusion of the fight. This storm seemed a signal from hell for the perpetration of villainy which would have ashamed the most ferocious barbarians of antiquity. The direst, the most revolting cruelty was added to the catalogue of crimes. One atrocity, of which a girl of seventeen was the victim, staggers the mind by its enormous, incredible, indescribable barbarity, and though many officers exerted themselves to preserve order, and many men were well conducted, the rapine and violence commenced by villains spread, the camp followers soon crowded into the place, and the disorder continued until the flames, following the steps of the plunderer, put an end to his ferocity by destroying the whole town.

The fall of San Sebastian had given Wellington a new port and point of support, and it seemed certain therefore that he would immediately invade France.

The country beyond the Bidassoa was sterile, and it would be difficult for him to feed his army there in winter. Soult's position at Bayonne and St. Jean Pied-de-Port was strong, his troops still numerous, and no serious invasion could be made until one or both were taken or blockaded.

On the 10th November, 1813, ninety thousand men of all arms, of whom seventy-four thousand were Anglo-Portuguese, and ninety-five guns, were brought into action with inconceivable vigour. Wellington, seeing that the right of Soult's line could not well be forced, designed to hold it in check, while he forced the centre and left and pushed down the Nivelle to San Pé.

The seventh division was now a part of Beresford's force, and was posted on the slopes of the Great Rhune Mountain. The weakest point of Soult's line was the opening between this mountain and the Nivelle. This space was the most open, and the least fortified, and the Nivelle was fordable above the bridge of Amotz.

The seventh division was to storm the Grenada redoubt and assail the enemy's position, by way of the village of Sarre. The troops advanced with scaling-ladders and the skirmishers got into the rear of the work, whereupon the French fled, and the division carried the village of Sarre. After the fall of the redoubt the French endeavoured to defend the heights of Sarre, but the fourth and seventh divisions, with the 94th Regiment, detached from the third division, pushed towards the bridge of Amotz, and the French fearing to be cut off from San Pé fell back in disorder from Sarrer closely pursued by the fourth and seventh divisions, until they stood firm in the redoubt Louis XIV. and were again assailed in front, when the redoubt was carried and the garrison bayoneted.

The French were now flying in disorder along the road to San Pé, but they made a final stand at the Signal redoubt. A portion of the seventh division here broke the 31st French Regiment,[9] which attempted to charge them, and the route was complete. The French fled to the different bridges over the Nivelle, and took post on some heights immediately above San Pé. Welling-

9. A French regiment consisted of three battalions, equal to a British Brigade.

ton then disposed of his divisions to force the passage of the Nivelle, and crossed himself with the third and seventh divisions and drove the enemy from his new position, in which Inglis was wounded and the regiments of his brigade handled very roughly. The enemy quitted all his works during the night, destroying the bridges in the lower Nivelle, and retired again during the night of the 11th into an entrenched camp in front of Bayonne.

During these operations the 82nd took part with the 51st and 68th in driving the enemy from the heights of San Pé, for which service the 51st and 68th alone were particularly mentioned in Lord Wellington's dispatches to Earl Bathurst, dated San Pé, 13th November, 1813, thus:

> I likewise particularly observed the gallant conduct of the 51st and 68th Regiments, in Major-General Inglis's brigade, in the attack on the heights above San Pé on the afternoon of the 10th.

This would appear to have arisen from a mistake in the report of the assistant adjutant-general attached to the division, who, in answer to a question as to what corps it was carrying the heights so gallantly, mentioned the above-named regiments, when it was, in fact, the 82nd that bore the brunt of the affair, after the other two regiments of the brigade, being very weak, had been checked. The 82nd lost on this day nine rank and file killed. Captain Marshall, Lieutenants Mortimer, Mason, Cuthbert, and Ensigns Sydserf and Whittaker, six sergeants, and sixty-eight rank and file wounded.

After the operations of the 10th November, the weather for some days was so wet and the roads so bad that all movements were prevented, and it was not till the 8th of December that Lord Wellington was able to move the troops from their cantonments and follow the enemy to Bayonne. A series of operations then ensued on both sides, connected with the passage of the Nive, in which the seventh division was not actively engaged.

After these operations the allied army remained inactive on account of the severity of the weather; and it was not till the middle of February, 1814, that the troops were again put in motion.

On the 23rd February, 1814, the brigade to which the 82nd was attached dislodged the enemy from a *tête-de-pont* at the fortified post of Oyergave, on the left of the Gave-de-pau, and obliged him to retire within the *tête-de-pont* of Peyrehorade. The 82nd suffered on this occasion a comparatively trifling loss—having but one officer,. Captain Carew, and two rank and file wounded. The whole army having passed the Gave d'Oleron moved towards Orthez, and within four miles of that city confronted Soult's army, when a decisive battle was fought, in which the 82nd again bore a conspicuous part.

The French army, having destroyed all the bridges, assembled near the town of Orthez, on the 25th February, 1814 A general attack was then ordered, which succeeded after a vigorous resistance. The 82nd was still in the seventh division, under Field Marshal Sir William Beresford, but the immediate command of the division was with Major-General Walker. The Marshal crossed the Gave-de-Pau on the 25th, below the junction of the Gave d'Oleron, and on the morning of the 26th moved along the high road from Peyrehorade towards Orthez. The other divisions crossed at daylight on the 27th. Beresford received Lord Wellington's orders to attack the enemy's right on the heights, on the high road to Dax. The course of these heights retired his centre and gave extraordinary strength to the flanks. Beresford carried the village of St. Boe's, after an obstinate resistance; but the ground was so narrow that the troops could not deploy to attack the heights, and it was found impossible to turn the right An attack was then made on the left, led by the 52nd, which succeeded in dislodging the enemy and forcing him to retreat in great confusion, leaving open the direct road towards Bordeaux. The allied army passed the Adour on the 1st March, and were—

> . . . . in possession of all the great communications across the river, after having beaten the enemy and " taken their magazines. All the troops distinguished themselves—the seventh division, under Major-General Walker, in the various operations and attacks during the enemy's retreat.[10]

10. Wellington's Despatches.

The 82nd lost in this action, Lieutenant-Colonel Conyers, wounded severely; Lieutenant Drummond, and thirty rank and file, wounded. Lieutenant-Colonel Conyers, and Major Vincent, who succeeded to the command towards the end of the action, were granted a medal commemorative of the victory, and the regiment received permission to bear "Orthez" on its colours and appointments. This was the last occasion on which the 82nd met the enemy in France, as the seventh division immediately afterwards took possession of Bordeaux. Here the first battalion received a draft of five sergeants and one hundred and twenty-nine rank and file, from the second battalion in Alderney.

On the 3rd May, 1814, the regiment embarked for North America at Pouillac, near Bordeaux, and after a fine passage arrived at Quebec, on the 25th June, whence it proceeded immediately up the country to Fort Erie, and there joined the right division of the army on the Niagara frontier.

## American War

On the 18th June, 1812, an Act was passed by the American Congress, declaring the actual existence of war between the United Kingdom of Great Britain and Ireland and the United States of America. By a late militia law of Canada a draft of two thousand men was to be made from the militia of the province for three months, in order to be trained and disciplined. The campaign against Canada commenced early in July, and a considerable force was assembled in the neighbourhood of Niagara. On the 13th October the British position at Queenstown Heights, on the Niagara river, was attacked, Major-General Brock hastened to the spot with reinforcements, and was unfortunately killed in the act of cheering on his men. Major-General Sheaffe, the next in command, brought up fresh troops, and after a sharp contest defeated the Americans.

Notwithstanding repeated failures the American Government persisted in its purpose of invading Canada, but no operations of consequence were undertaken during the remainder of the year.

On the 30th March, 1813, a public notification was issued by the Prince Regent that measures had been taken for blockading the ports and harbours of New York, Charleston, Port Royal, Savannah, and the River Mississippi, as well as the Chesapeake and Delaware rivers. On the 22nd February the Americans at Ogdensburgh had been attacked by a force from Prescot, and the place was carried; but on the 27th April, York (now Toronto), the capital of Upper Canada, on Lake Ontario, was captured by the enemy. On the 27th May, Fort George, at the mouth of the Niagara river, was taken by a powerful force, and though very gallantly opposed by Colonel Vincent, the superiority of the enemy's numbers obliged the British commander to evacuate the place and retire towards the head of Lake Ontario. The American army then pushed on towards Queenstown, and with ten thousand men became complete masters of the Niagara frontier. Before the year closed, however, the British surprised and captured Fort Niagara, taking twenty-seven pieces of ordnance and about three thousand stand of arms, with clothing, camp equipage, &c; and the Americans, having so far failed in their invasion of the Provinces, were obliged to retire into winter quarters within their own territory.

A large American force, computed at six thousand men, under Major-General Brown, crossed the Niagara river on the 3rd July, 1814, and advanced into Canada, driving before them the British piquets at Fort Erie. They then proceeded to the lines of Chippewa, when Major-General Riall went out to meet them, with one thousand five hundred regular troops, besides militia and Indians, but the British were forced to retreat to a position near Fort Niagara.

On the 25th July an action was fought at Lundy's Lane, near the Falls of Niagara, by General Drummond. This action continued from six o'clock in the evening to nine. The efforts of the enemy were renewed till midnight, when he gave up the contest and retired to Fort Erie.

The arrival of succours from Lord Wellington's army in the Peninsula and this defeat were timely events. General Drummond opened a battery, on the 13th August, against Fort Erie, and assaulted it on the 15th before daylight at two different points. Both assaults unfortunately failed, owing to the explosion of a magazine, by which all the men who had entered the place were dreadfully mangled. The attack was then abandoned, and the general retired to his battery, with a loss of nine hundred and sixty-two officers and men. Immediately after this repulse the 82nd Regiment joined his division. Sir George Prevost, in a despatch to Earl Bathurst, dated Montreal, 27th August, 1814, writes:

> By accounts from Lieutenant-General Drummond, to the 18th instant, I find he has since the 15th been joined by the 82nd Regiment.

On the 25th August the enemy made a sortie from Fort Erie, which was repulsed, when the 82nd were for the first time engaged and lost four rank and file killed, one rank and file wounded, besides several men hit by buckshot, whose names were not included in the returns.

On the 17th September the British batteries were again attacked by the enemy from Fort Erie, with a large proportion of his force, but he was again repulsed with great loss by the intrepid bravery of General Drummond's division, which is thus described in Major-General Wattevelle's despatch:

> Camp before Fort Erie
> September 19,1814
> The enemy attacked our position on the 17th, in the afternoon, under cover of a heavy fire of his artillery from Fort Erie, and, much favoured by the nature of the ground and the rain falling in torrents, he succeeded in turning the right of our line of piquets unperceived, and with a very considerable force attacked both the piquets and supports in flank and rear. At the same time another column attacked in front the piquet between No. 2 and No. 3 Batteries, and though delayed considerably by the obstinate resistance made by the piquets under every pos-

> sible disadvantage, he at last succeeded in getting possession of both the batteries. As soon as the alarm was given the first brigade, composed of the Royal Scots, the 82nd and 89th Regiments, under Lieutenant-Colonel Gordon, received orders to march forward, the 6th Regiment remaining in reserve under Lieutenant-Colonel Campbell. The Royals and 89th engaged the enemy on the right of No. 3 Battery, and checked his farther progress. The 82nd and three companies of the 6th were detached to the left to support Nos. 1 and 2 Batteries, the enemy having at that time possession of No. 2 Battery, and still pushing forward. Seven companies of the 82nd, under Major Proctor, and three companies of the 6th, under Major Taylor, immediately charged him with the most intrepid bravery, driving him back across our entrenchments and also from No. 2 Battery.

Lieutenant-General Drummond also bears witness to the dash and gallantry of the 82nd, in these words:

> The charge made by the 82nd Regiment, under Major Proctor, and detachment of the 6th, under Major Taylor, led to the recovery of the Battery No. 2, and very much decided the precipitate retrograde movement made by the enemy from the different points of our position of which he had gained short possession.

The enemy being thus repulsed at every point, was forced to retire with precipitation to his works, and by five o'clock the line of piquets was re-established as it had been previous to the attack. The British loss on this occasion was some six hundred in killed, wounded, and missing, while the 82nd alone lost Captain Wright and Ensign Langford, two sergeants, three corporals, and six men killed; Captain Marshall, Lieutenants Pigot, Latham, Mason, Harman, and seven men wounded.

By the 24th September the troops had taken up their cantonments behind French Creek, and were in comfortable winter quarters.

The commissioners of the contending powers had been actively engaged in Europe in negotiations for the restoration of peace, and a treaty was signed at Ghent, on the 24th December, between His Majesty and the United States of America.

In the month of January, 1815, the first battalion received five sergeants and one hundred and twenty rank and file from the second battalion. On the 16th June the first battalion left the Niagara frontier, on its way to the Lower Province, and embarked on the 28th June, at Quebec, for England. It landed at Portsmouth, and three days afterwards proceeded to Ostend. The Establishment was now reduced by an order from the War Office, dated 3rd April, 1815, to fifty sergeants and one thousand rank and file. On the 9th August the regiment landed at Ostend, and marched to join the Duke of Wellington in Paris, where it arrived in twenty-five days, and encamped on the plains of St. Denis.

On the 15th September it received a draft of two sergeants and one hundred and nine men from the second battalion, quartered since the middle of last month at Fort Moncton, near Gosport. In justice to this second battalion, which made every sacrifice to uphold the fame of the first, the following extract is added from the Adjutant-General's Office, dated Horse Guards, 10th August, 1813:

82nd Regiment
2nd Battalion
The Commander-in-Chief was pleased to express his satisfaction at the report of this corps, so favourable to its discipline and interior economy.
(Signed) *H. Calvert*
A. General
Lieutenant-General Sir John Doyle, &c., &c., &c.
A true copy.
(Signed) *Daire Lacy* M. B.
Major Conyers
Commanding 2nd Battalion
82nd Regiment

# ALSO FROM LEONAUR

## AVAILABLE IN SOFTCOVER OR HARDCOVER WITH DUST JACKET

**A HISTORY OF THE FRENCH & INDIAN WAR** *by Arthur G. Bradley*—The Seven Years War as it was fought in the New World has always fascinated students of military history—here is the story of that confrontation.

**WASHINGTON'S EARLY CAMPAIGNS** *by James Hadden*—The French Post Expedition, Great Meadows and Braddock's Defeat—including Braddock's Orderly Books.

**BOUQUET & THE OHIO INDIAN WAR** *by Cyrus Cort & William Smith*—Two Accounts of the Campaigns of 1763-1764: Bouquet's Campaigns by Cyrus Cort & The History of Bouquet's Expeditions by William Smith.

**NARRATIVES OF THE FRENCH & INDIAN WAR: 2** *by David Holden, Samuel Jenks, Lemuel Lyon, Mary Cochrane Rogers & Henry T. Blake*—Contains The Diary of Sergeant David Holden, Captain Samuel Jenks' Journal, The Journal of Lemuel Lyon, Journal of a French Officer at the Siege of Quebec, A Battle Fought on Snowshoes & The Battle of Lake George.

**NARRATIVES OF THE FRENCH & INDIAN WAR** *by Brown, Eastburn, Hawks & Putnam*—Ranger Brown's Narrative, The Adventures of Robert Eastburn, The Journal of Rufus Putnam—Provincial Infantry & Orderly Book and Journal of Major John Hawks on the Ticonderoga-Crown Point Campaign.

**THE 7TH (QUEEN'S OWN) HUSSARS: Volume 1: 1688-1792** *by C. R. B. Barrett*—As Dragoons During the Flanders Campaign, War of the Austrian Succession and the Seven Years War

**INDIA'S FREE LANCES** *by H. G. Keene*—European Mercenary Commanders in Hindustan 1770-1820.

**THE BENGAL EUROPEAN REGIMENT** *by P. R. Innes*—An Elite Regiment of the Honourable East India Company 1756-1858.

**MUSKET & TOMAHAWK** *by Francis Parkman*—A Military History of the French & Indian War, 1753-1760.

**THE BLACK WATCH AT TICONDEROGA** *by Frederick B. Richards*—Campaigns in the French & Indian War.

**QUEEN'S RANGERS** *by Frederick B. Richards*—John Simcoe and his Rangers During the Revolutionary War for America.

# ALSO FROM LEONAUR

## AVAILABLE IN SOFTCOVER OR HARDCOVER WITH DUST JACKET

**JOURNALS OF ROBERT ROGERS OF THE RANGERS** *by Robert Rogers*—The exploits of Rogers & the Rangers in his own words during 1755-1761 in the French & Indian War.

**GALLOPING GUNS** *by James Young*—The Experiences of an Officer of the Bengal Horse Artillery During the Second Maratha War 1804-1805.

**GORDON** *by Demetrius Charles Boulger*—The Career of Gordon of Khartoum.

**THE BATTLE OF NEW ORLEANS** *by Zachary F. Smith*—The final major engagement of the War of 1812.

**THE TWO WARS OF MRS DUBERLY** *by Frances Isabella Duberly*—An Intrepid Victorian Lady's Experience of the Crimea and Indian Mutiny.

**WITH THE GUARDS' BRIGADE DURING THE BOER WAR** *by Edward P. Lowry*—On Campaign from Bloemfontein to Koomati Poort and Back.

**THE REBELLIOUS DUCHESS** *by Paul F. S. Dermoncourt*—The Adventures of the Duchess of Berri and Her Attempt to Overthrow French Monarchy.

**MEN OF THE MUTINY** *by John Tulloch Nash & Henry Metcalfe*—Two Accounts of the Great Indian Mutiny of 1857: Fighting with the Bengal Yeomanry Cavalry & Private Metcalfe at Lucknow.

**CAMPAIGN IN THE CRIMEA** *by George Shuldham Peard*—The Recollections of an Officer of the 20th Regiment of Foot.

**WITHIN SEBASTOPOL** *by K. Hodasevich*—A Narrative of the Campaign in the Crimea, and of the Events of the Siege.

**WITH THE CAVALRY TO AFGHANISTAN** *by William Taylor*—The Experiences of a Trooper of H. M. 4th Light Dragoons During the First Afghan War.

**THE CAWNPORE MAN** *by Mowbray Thompson*—A First Hand Account of the Siege and Massacre During the Indian Mutiny By One of Four Survivors.

**BRIGADE COMMANDER: AFGHANISTAN** *by Henry Brooke*—The Journal of the Commander of the 2nd Infantry Brigade, Kandahar Field Force During the Second Afghan War.

**BANCROFT OF THE BENGAL HORSE ARTILLERY** *by N. W. Bancroft*—An Account of the First Sikh War 1845-1846.

# ALSO FROM LEONAUR

## AVAILABLE IN SOFTCOVER OR HARDCOVER WITH DUST JACKET

**AFGHANISTAN: THE BELEAGUERED BRIGADE** *by G. R. Gleig*—An Account of Sale's Brigade During the First Afghan War.

**IN THE RANKS OF THE C. I. V** *by Erskine Childers*—With the City Imperial Volunteer Battery (Honourable Artillery Company) in the Second Boer War.

**THE BENGAL NATIVE ARMY** *by F. G. Cardew*—An Invaluable Reference Resource.

**THE 7TH (QUEEN'S OWN) HUSSARS** *by C. R. B. Barrett*—Uniforms, Equipment, Weapons, Traditions, the Services of Notable Officers and Men & the Appendices to All Volumes—Volume 4 1688-1914.

**THE SWORD OF THE CROWN** *by Eric W. Sheppard*—A History of the British Army to 1914.

**THE 7TH (QUEEN'S OWN) HUSSARS** *by C. R. B. Barrett*—On Campaign During the Canadian Rebellion, the Indian Mutiny, the Sudan, Matabeleland, Mashonaland and the Boer War Volume 3: 1818-1914.

**THE KHARTOUM CAMPAIGN** *by Bennet Burleigh*—A Special Correspondent's View of the Reconquest of the Sudan by British and Egyptian Forces under Kitchener—1898.

**EL PUCHERO** *by Richard McSherry*—The Letters of a Surgeon of Volunteers During Scott's Campaign of the American-Mexican War 1847-1848.

**RIFLEMAN SAHIB** *by E. Maude*—The Recollections of an Officer of the Bombay Rifles During the Southern Mahratta Campaign, Second Sikh War, Persian Campaign and Indian Mutiny.

**THE KING'S HUSSAR** *by Edwin Mole*—The Recollections of a 14th (King's) Hussar During the Victorian Era.

**JOHN COMPANY'S CAVALRYMAN** *by William Johnson*—The Experiences of a British Soldier in the Crimea, the Persian Campaign and the Indian Mutiny.

**COLENSO & DURNFORD'S ZULU WAR** *by Frances E. Colenso & Edward Durnford*—The first and possibly the most important history of the Zulu War.

**U. S. DRAGOON** *by Samuel E. Chamberlain*—Experiences in the Mexican War 1846-48 and on the South Western Frontier.

# ALSO FROM LEONAUR

## AVAILABLE IN SOFTCOVER OR HARDCOVER WITH DUST JACKET

**THE 2ND MAORI WAR: 1860-1861** *by Robert Carey*—The Second Maori War, or First Taranaki War, one more bloody instalment of the conflicts between European settlers and the indigenous Maori people.

**A JOURNAL OF THE SECOND SIKH WAR** *by Daniel A. Sandford*—The Experiences of an Ensign of the 2nd Bengal European Regiment During the Campaign in the Punjab, India, 1848-49.

**THE LIGHT INFANTRY OFFICER** *by John H. Cooke*—The Experiences of an Officer of the 43rd Light Infantry in America During the War of 1812.

**BUSHVELDT CARBINEERS** *by George Witton*—The War Against the Boers in South Africa and the 'Breaker' Morant Incident.

**LAKE'S CAMPAIGNS IN INDIA** *by Hugh Pearse*—The Second Anglo Maratha War, 1803-1807.

**BRITAIN IN AFGHANISTAN 1: THE FIRST AFGHAN WAR 1839-42** *by Archibald Forbes*—From invasion to destruction-a British military disaster.

**BRITAIN IN AFGHANISTAN 2: THE SECOND AFGHAN WAR 1878-80** *by Archibald Forbes*—This is the history of the Second Afghan War-another episode of British military history typified by savagery, massacre, siege and battles.

**UP AMONG THE PANDIES** *by Vivian Dering Majendie*—Experiences of a British Officer on Campaign During the Indian Mutiny, 1857-1858.

**MUTINY: 1857** *by James Humphries*—Authentic Voices from the Indian Mutiny-First Hand Accounts of Battles, Sieges and Personal Hardships.

**BLOW THE BUGLE, DRAW THE SWORD** *by W. H. G. Kingston*—The Wars, Campaigns, Regiments and Soldiers of the British & Indian Armies During the Victorian Era, 1839-1898.

**WAR BEYOND THE DRAGON PAGODA** *by Major J. J. Snodgrass*—A Personal Narrative of the First Anglo-Burmese War 1824 - 1826.

**THE HERO OF ALIWAL** *by James Humphries*—The Campaigns of Sir Harry Smith in India, 1843-1846, During the Gwalior War & the First Sikh War.

**ALL FOR A SHILLING A DAY** *by Donald F. Featherstone*—The story of H.M. 16th, the Queen's Lancers During the first Sikh War 1845-1846.

# ALSO FROM LEONAUR

## AVAILABLE IN SOFTCOVER OR HARDCOVER WITH DUST JACKET

**THE FALL OF THE MOGHUL EMPIRE OF HINDUSTAN** *by H. G. Keene*—By the beginning of the nineteenth century, as British and Indian armies under Lake and Wellesley dominated the scene, a little over half a century of conflict brought the Moghul Empire to its knees.

**LADY SALE'S AFGHANISTAN** *by Florentia Sale*—An Indomitable Victorian Lady's Account of the Retreat from Kabul During the First Afghan War.

**THE CAMPAIGN OF MAGENTA AND SOLFERINO 1859** *by Harold Carmichael Wylly*—The Decisive Conflict for the Unification of Italy.

**FRENCH'S CAVALRY CAMPAIGN** *by J. G. Maydon*—A Special Correspondent's View of British Army Mounted Troops During the Boer War.

**CAVALRY AT WATERLOO** *by Sir Evelyn Wood*—British Mounted Troops During the Campaign of 1815.

**THE SUBALTERN** *by George Robert Gleig*—The Experiences of an Officer of the 85th Light Infantry During the Peninsular War.

**NAPOLEON AT BAY, 1814** *by F. Loraine Petre*—The Campaigns to the Fall of the First Empire.

**NAPOLEON AND THE CAMPAIGN OF 1806** *by Colonel Vachée*—The Napoleonic Method of Organisation and Command to the Battles of Jena & Auerstädt.

**THE COMPLETE ADVENTURES IN THE CONNAUGHT RANGERS** *by William Grattan*—The 88th Regiment during the Napoleonic Wars by a Serving Officer.

**BUGLER AND OFFICER OF THE RIFLES** *by William Green & Harry Smith*—With the 95th (Rifles) during the Peninsular & Waterloo Campaigns of the Napoleonic Wars.

**NAPOLEONIC WAR STORIES** *by Sir Arthur Quiller-Couch*—Tales of soldiers, spies, battles & sieges from the Peninsular & Waterloo campaingns.

**CAPTAIN OF THE 95TH (RIFLES)** *by Jonathan Leach*—An officer of Wellington's sharpshooters during the Peninsular, South of France and Waterloo campaigns of the Napoleonic wars.

**RIFLEMAN COSTELLO** *by Edward Costello*—The adventures of a soldier of the 95th (Rifles) in the Peninsular & Waterloo Campaigns of the Napoleonic wars.

LEONAUR

# ALSO FROM LEONAUR

## AVAILABLE IN SOFTCOVER OR HARDCOVER WITH DUST JACKET

**ZULU:1879** *by D.C.F. Moodie & the Leonaur Editors*—The Anglo-Zulu War of 1879 from contemporary sources: First Hand Accounts, Interviews, Dispatches, Official Documents & Newspaper Reports.

**THE RED DRAGOON** *by W.J. Adams*—With the 7th Dragoon Guards in the Cape of Good Hope against the Boers & the Kaffir tribes during the 'war of the axe' 1843-48'.

**THE RECOLLECTIONS OF SKINNER OF SKINNER'S HORSE** *by James Skinner*—James Skinner and his 'Yellow Boys' Irregular cavalry in the wars of India between the British, Mahratta, Rajput, Mogul, Sikh & Pindarree Forces.

**A CAVALRY OFFICER DURING THE SEPOY REVOLT** *by A. R. D. Mackenzie*—Experiences with the 3rd Bengal Light Cavalry, the Guides and Sikh Irregular Cavalry from the outbreak to Delhi and Lucknow.

**A NORFOLK SOLDIER IN THE FIRST SIKH WAR** *by J W Baldwin*—Experiences of a private of H.M. 9th Regiment of Foot in the battles for the Punjab, India 1845-6.

**TOMMY ATKINS' WAR STORIES: 14 FIRST HAND ACCOUNTS**—Fourteen first hand accounts from the ranks of the British Army during Queen Victoria's Empire.

**THE WATERLOO LETTERS** *by H. T. Siborne*—Accounts of the Battle by British Officers for its Foremost Historian.

**NEY: GENERAL OF CAVALRY VOLUME 1—1769-1799** *by Antoine Bulos*—The Early Career of a Marshal of the First Empire.

**NEY: MARSHAL OF FRANCE VOLUME 2—1799-1805** *by Antoine Bulos*—The Early Career of a Marshal of the First Empire.

**AIDE-DE-CAMP TO NAPOLEON** *by Philippe-Paul de Ségur*—For anyone interested in the Napoleonic Wars this book, written by one who was intimate with the strategies and machinations of the Emperor, will be essential reading.

**TWILIGHT OF EMPIRE** *by Sir Thomas Ussher & Sir George Cockburn*—Two accounts of Napoleon's Journeys in Exile to Elba and St. Helena: Narrative of Events by Sir Thomas Ussher & Napoleon's Last Voyage: Extract of a diary by Sir George Cockburn.

**PRIVATE WHEELER** *by William Wheeler*—The letters of a soldier of the 51st Light Infantry during the Peninsular War & at Waterloo.

# ALSO FROM LEONAUR

## AVAILABLE IN SOFTCOVER OR HARDCOVER WITH DUST JACKET

**OFFICERS & GENTLEMEN** *by Peter Hawker & William Graham*—Two Accounts of British Officers During the Peninsula War: Officer of Light Dragoons by Peter Hawker & Campaign in Portugal and Spain by William Graham .

**THE WALCHEREN EXPEDITION** *by Anonymous*—The Experiences of a British Officer of the 81st Regt. During the Campaign in the Low Countries of 1809.

**LADIES OF WATERLOO** *by Charlotte A. Eaton, Magdalene de Lancey & Juana Smith*—The Experiences of Three Women During the Campaign of 1815: Waterloo Days by Charlotte A. Eaton, A Week at Waterloo by Magdalene de Lancey & Juana's Story by Juana Smith.

**JOURNAL OF AN OFFICER IN THE KING'S GERMAN LEGION** *by John Frederick Hering*—Recollections of Campaigning During the Napoleonic Wars.

**JOURNAL OF AN ARMY SURGEON IN THE PENINSULAR WAR** *by Charles Boutflower*—The Recollections of a British Army Medical Man on Campaign During the Napoleonic Wars.

**ON CAMPAIGN WITH MOORE AND WELLINGTON** *by Anthony Hamilton*—The Experiences of a Soldier of the 43rd Regiment During the Peninsular War.

**THE ROAD TO AUSTERLITZ** *by R. G. Burton*—Napoleon's Campaign of 1805.

**SOLDIERS OF NAPOLEON** *by A. J. Doisy De Villargennes & Arthur Chuquet*—The Experiences of the Men of the French First Empire: Under the Eagles by A. J. Doisy De Villargennes & Voices of 1812 by Arthur Chuquet .

**INVASION OF FRANCE, 1814** *by F. W. O. Maycock*—The Final Battles of the Napoleonic First Empire.

**LEIPZIG—A CONFLICT OF TITANS** *by Frederic Shoberl*—A Personal Experience of the 'Battle of the Nations' During the Napoleonic Wars, October 14th-19th, 1813.

**SLASHERS** *by Charles Cadell*—The Campaigns of the 28th Regiment of Foot During the Napoleonic Wars by a Serving Officer.

**BATTLE IMPERIAL** *by Charles William Vane*—The Campaigns in Germany & France for the Defeat of Napoleon 1813-1814.

**SWIFT & BOLD** *by Gibbes Rigaud*—The 60th Rifles During the Peninsula War.

AVAILABLE ONLINE AT **www.leonaur.com**
AND FROM ALL GOOD BOOK STORES

07/09

# ALSO FROM LEONAUR

**AVAILABLE IN SOFTCOVER OR HARDCOVER WITH DUST JACKET**

**ADVENTURES OF A YOUNG RIFLEMAN** *by Johann Christian Maempel*—The Experiences of a Saxon in the French & British Armies During the Napoleonic Wars.

**THE HUSSAR** *by Norbert Landsheit & G. R. Gleig*—A German Cavalryman in British Service Throughout the Napoleonic Wars.

**RECOLLECTIONS OF THE PENINSULA** *by Moyle Sherer*—An Officer of the 34th Regiment of Foot—'The Cumberland Gentlemen'—on Campaign Against Napoleon's French Army in Spain.

**MARINE OF REVOLUTION & CONSULATE** *by Moreau de Jonnès*—The Recollections of a French Soldier of the Revolutionary Wars 1791-1804.

**GENTLEMEN IN RED** *by John Dobbs & Robert Knowles*—Two Accounts of British Infantry Officers During the Peninsular War Recollections of an Old 52nd Man by John Dobbs An Officer of Fusiliers by Robert Knowles.

**CORPORAL BROWN'S CAMPAIGNS IN THE LOW COUNTRIES** *by Robert Brown*—Recollections of a Coldstream Guard in the Early Campaigns Against Revolutionary France 1793-1795.

**THE 7TH (QUEENS OWN) HUSSARS** *by C. R. B. Barrett*—During the Campaigns in the Low Countries & the Peninsula and Waterloo Campaigns of the Napoleonic Wars. Volume 2: 1793-1815.

**THE MARENGO CAMPAIGN 1800** *by Herbert H. Sargent*—The Victory that Completed the Austrian Defeat in Italy.

**DONALDSON OF THE 94TH—SCOTS BRIGADE** *by Joseph Donaldson*—The Recollections of a Soldier During the Peninsula & South of France Campaigns of the Napoleonic Wars.

**A CONSCRIPT FOR EMPIRE** *by Philippe as told to Johann Christian Maempel*—The Experiences of a Young German Conscript During the Napoleonic Wars.

**JOURNAL OF THE CAMPAIGN OF 1815** *by Alexander Cavalié Mercer*—The Experiences of an Officer of the Royal Horse Artillery During the Waterloo Campaign.

**NAPOLEON'S CAMPAIGNS IN POLAND 1806-7** *by Robert Wilson*—The campaign in Poland from the Russian side of the conflict.

# ALSO FROM LEONAUR

## AVAILABLE IN SOFTCOVER OR HARDCOVER WITH DUST JACKET

**OMPTEDA OF THE KING'S GERMAN LEGION** *by Christian von Ompteda*—A Hanoverian Officer on Campaign Against Napoleon.

**LIEUTENANT SIMMONS OF THE 95TH (RIFLES)** *by George Simmons*—Recollections of the Peninsula, South of France & Waterloo Campaigns of the Napoleonic Wars.

**A HORSEMAN FOR THE EMPEROR** *by Jean Baptiste Gazzola*—A Cavalryman of Napoleon's Army on Campaign Throughout the Napoleonic Wars.

**SERGEANT LAWRENCE** *by William Lawrence*—With the 40th Regt. of Foot in South America, the Peninsular War & at Waterloo.

**CAMPAIGNS WITH THE FIELD TRAIN** *by Richard D. Henegan*—Experiences of a British Officer During the Peninsula and Waterloo Campaigns of the Napoleonic Wars.

**CAVALRY SURGEON** *by S. D. Broughton*—On Campaign Against Napoleon in the Peninsula & South of France During the Napoleonic Wars 1812-1814.

**MEN OF THE RIFLES** *by Thomas Knight, Henry Curling & Jonathan Leach*—The Reminiscences of Thomas Knight of the 95th (Rifles) by Thomas Knight, Henry Curling's Anecdotes by Henry Curling & The Field Services of the Rifle Brigade from its Formation to Waterloo by Jonathan Leach.

**THE ULM CAMPAIGN 1805** *by F. N. Maude*—Napoleon and the Defeat of the Austrian Army During the 'War of the Third Coalition'.

**SOLDIERING WITH THE 'DIVISION'** *by Thomas Garrety*—The Military Experiences of an Infantryman of the 43rd Regiment During the Napoleonic Wars.

**SERGEANT MORRIS OF THE 73RD FOOT** *by Thomas Morris*—The Experiences of a British Infantryman During the Napoleonic Wars-Including Campaigns in Germany and at Waterloo.

**A VOICE FROM WATERLOO** *by Edward Cotton*—The Personal Experiences of a British Cavalryman Who Became a Battlefield Guide and Authority on the Campaign of 1815.

**NAPOLEON AND HIS MARSHALS** *by J. T. Headley*—The Men of the First Empire.

# ALSO FROM LEONAUR

## AVAILABLE IN SOFTCOVER OR HARDCOVER WITH DUST JACKET

**COLBORNE: A SINGULAR TALENT FOR WAR** *by John Colborne*—The Napoleonic Wars Career of One of Wellington's Most Highly Valued Officers in Egypt, Holland, Italy, the Peninsula and at Waterloo.

**NAPOLEON'S RUSSIAN CAMPAIGN** *by Philippe Henri de Segur*—The Invasion, Battles and Retreat by an Aide-de-Camp on the Emperor's Staff.

**WITH THE LIGHT DIVISION** *by John H. Cooke*—The Experiences of an Officer of the 43rd Light Infantry in the Peninsula and South of France During the Napoleonic Wars.

**WELLINGTON AND THE PYRENEES CAMPAIGN VOLUME I: FROM VITORIA TO THE BIDASSOA** *by F. C. Beatson*—The final phase of the campaign in the Iberian Peninsula.

**WELLINGTON AND THE INVASION OF FRANCE VOLUME II: THE BIDASSOA TO THE BATTLE OF THE NIVELLE** *by F. C. Beatson*—The final phase of the campaign in the Iberian Peninsula.

**WELLINGTON AND THE FALL OF FRANCE VOLUME III: THE GAVES AND THE BATTLE OF ORTHEZ** *by F. C. Beatson*—The final phase of the campaign in the Iberian Peninsula.

**NAPOLEON'S IMPERIAL GUARD: FROM MARENGO TO WATERLOO** *by J. T. Headley*—The story of Napoleon's Imperial Guard and the men who commanded them.

**BATTLES & SIEGES OF THE PENINSULAR WAR** *by W. H. Fitchett*—Corunna, Busaco, Albuera, Ciudad Rodrigo, Badajos, Salamanca, San Sebastian & Others.

**SERGEANT GUILLEMARD: THE MAN WHO SHOT NELSON?** *by Robert Guillemard*—A Soldier of the Infantry of the French Army of Napoleon on Campaign Throughout Europe.

**WITH THE GUARDS ACROSS THE PYRENEES** *by Robert Batty*—The Experiences of a British Officer of Wellington's Army During the Battles for the Fall of Napoleonic France, 1813 .

**A STAFF OFFICER IN THE PENINSULA** *by E. W. Buckham*—An Officer of the British Staff Corps Cavalry During the Peninsula Campaign of the Napoleonic Wars.

**THE LEIPZIG CAMPAIGN: 1813—NAPOLEON AND THE "BATTLE OF THE NATIONS"** *by F. N. Maude*—Colonel Maude's analysis of Napoleon's campaign of 1813 around Leipzig.

# ALSO FROM LEONAUR

## AVAILABLE IN SOFTCOVER OR HARDCOVER WITH DUST JACKET

**CAPTAIN COIGNET** *by Jean-Roch Coignet*—A Soldier of Napoleon's Imperial Guard from the Italian Campaign to Russia and Waterloo.

**HUSSAR ROCCA** *by Albert Jean Michel de Rocca*—A French cavalry officer's experiences of the Napoleonic Wars and his views on the Peninsular Campaigns against the Spanish, British And Guerilla Armies.

**MARINES TO 95TH (RIFLES)** *by Thomas Fernyhough*—The military experiences of Robert Fernyhough during the Napoleonic Wars.

**LIGHT BOB** *by Robert Blakeney*—The experiences of a young officer in H.M 28th & 36th regiments of the British Infantry during the Peninsular Campaign of the Napoleonic Wars 1804 - 1814.

**WITH WELLINGTON'S LIGHT CAVALRY** *by William Tomkinson*—The Experiences of an officer of the 16th Light Dragoons in the Peninsular and Waterloo campaigns of the Napoleonic Wars.

**SERGEANT BOURGOGNE** *by Adrien Bourgogne*—With Napoleon's Imperial Guard in the Russian Campaign and on the Retreat from Moscow 1812 - 13.

**SURTEES OF THE 95TH (RIFLES)** *by William Surtees*—A Soldier of the 95th (Rifles) in the Peninsular campaign of the Napoleonic Wars.

**SWORDS OF HONOUR** *by Henry Newbolt & Stanley L. Wood*—The Careers of Six Outstanding Officers from the Napoleonic Wars, the Wars for India and the American Civil War.

**ENSIGN BELL IN THE PENINSULAR WAR** *by George Bell*—The Experiences of a young British Soldier of the 34th Regiment 'The Cumberland Gentlemen' in the Napoleonic wars.

**HUSSAR IN WINTER** *by Alexander Gordon*—A British Cavalry Officer during the retreat to Corunna in the Peninsular campaign of the Napoleonic Wars.

**THE COMPLEAT RIFLEMAN HARRIS** *by Benjamin Harris as told to and transcribed by Captain Henry Curling, 52nd Regt. of Foot*—The adventures of a soldier of the 95th (Rifles) during the Peninsular Campaign of the Napoleonic Wars.

**THE ADVENTURES OF A LIGHT DRAGOON** *by George Farmer & G.R. Gleig*—A cavalryman during the Peninsular & Waterloo Campaigns, in captivity & at the siege of Bhurtpore, India.

# ALSO FROM LEONAUR

## AVAILABLE IN SOFTCOVER OR HARDCOVER WITH DUST JACKET

**THE LIFE OF THE REAL BRIGADIER GERARD VOLUME 1—THE YOUNG HUSSAR 1782-1807** *by Jean-Baptiste De Marbot*—A French Cavalryman Of the Napoleonic Wars at Marengo, Austerlitz, Jena, Eylau & Friedland.

**THE LIFE OF THE REAL BRIGADIER GERARD VOLUME 2—IMPERIAL AIDE-DE-CAMP 1807-1811** *by Jean-Baptiste De Marbot*—A French Cavalryman of the Napoleonic Wars at Saragossa, Landshut, Eckmuhl, Ratisbon, Aspern-Essling, Wagram, Busaco & Torres Vedras.

**THE LIFE OF THE REAL BRIGADIER GERARD VOLUME 3—COLONEL OF CHASSEURS 1811-1815** *by Jean-Baptiste De Marbot*—A French Cavalryman in the retreat from Moscow, Lutzen, Bautzen, Katzbach, Leipzig, Hanau & Waterloo.

**THE INDIAN WAR OF 1864** *by Eugene Ware*—The Experiences of a Young Officer of the 7th Iowa Cavalry on the Western Frontier During the Civil War.

**THE MARCH OF DESTINY** *by Charles E. Young & V. Devinny*—Dangers of the Trail in 1865 by Charles E. Young & The Story of a Pioneer by V. Devinny, two Accounts of Early Emigrants to Colorado.

**CROSSING THE PLAINS** *by William Audley Maxwell*—A First Hand Narrative of the Early Pioneer Trail to California in 1857.

**CHIEF OF SCOUTS** *by William F. Drannan*—A Pilot to Emigrant and Government Trains, Across the Plains of the Western Frontier.

**THIRTY-ONE YEARS ON THE PLAINS AND IN THE MOUNTAINS** *by William F. Drannan*—William Drannan was born to be a pioneer, hunter, trapper and wagon train guide during the momentous days of the Great American West.

**THE INDIAN WARS VOLUNTEER** *by William Thompson*—Recollections of the Conflict Against the Snakes, Shoshone, Bannocks, Modocs and Other Native Tribes of the American North West.

**THE 4TH TENNESSEE CAVALRY** *by George B. Guild*—The Services of Smith's Regiment of Confederate Cavalry by One of its Officers.

**COLONEL WORTHINGTON'S SHILOH** *by T. Worthington*—The Tennessee Campaign, 1862, by an Officer of the Ohio Volunteers.

**FOUR YEARS IN THE SADDLE** *by W. L. Curry*—The History of the First Regiment Ohio Volunteer Cavalry in the American Civil War.

# ALSO FROM LEONAUR

## AVAILABLE IN SOFTCOVER OR HARDCOVER WITH DUST JACKET

**THE RELUCTANT REBEL** *by William G. Stevenson*—A young Kentuckian's experiences in the Confederate Infantry & Cavalry during the American Civil War..

**BOOTS AND SADDLES** *by Elizabeth B. Custer*—The experiences of General Custer's Wife on the Western Plains.

**FANNIE BEERS' CIVIL WAR** *by Fannie A. Beers*—A Confederate Lady's Experiences of Nursing During the Campaigns & Battles of the American Civil War.

**LADY SALE'S AFGHANISTAN** *by Florentia Sale*—An Indomitable Victorian Lady's Account of the Retreat from Kabul During the First Afghan War.

**THE TWO WARS OF MRS DUBERLY** *by Frances Isabella Duberly*—An Intrepid Victorian Lady's Experience of the Crimea and Indian Mutiny.

**THE REBELLIOUS DUCHESS** *by Paul F. S. Dermoncourt*—The Adventures of the Duchess of Berri and Her Attempt to Overthrow French Monarchy.

**LADIES OF WATERLOO** *by Charlotte A. Eaton, Magdalene de Lancey & Juana Smith*—The Experiences of Three Women During the Campaign of 1815: Waterloo Days by Charlotte A. Eaton, A Week at Waterloo by Magdalene de Lancey & Juana's Story by Juana Smith.

**TWO YEARS BEFORE THE MAST** *by Richard Henry Dana. Jr.*—The account of one young man's experiences serving on board a sailing brig—the Penelope—bound for California, between the years1834-36.

**A SAILOR OF KING GEORGE** *by Frederick Hoffman*—From Midshipman to Captain—Recollections of War at Sea in the Napoleonic Age 1793-1815.

**LORDS OF THE SEA** *by A. T. Mahan*—Great Captains of the Royal Navy During the Age of Sail.

**COGGESHALL'S VOYAGES: VOLUME 1** *by George Coggeshall*—The Recollections of an American Schooner Captain.

**COGGESHALL'S VOYAGES: VOLUME 2** *by George Coggeshall*—The Recollections of an American Schooner Captain.

**TWILIGHT OF EMPIRE** *by Sir Thomas Ussher & Sir George Cockburn*—Two accounts of Napoleon's Journeys in Exile to Elba and St. Helena: Narrative of Events by Sir Thomas Ussher & Napoleon's Last Voyage: Extract of a diary by Sir George Cockburn.

AVAILABLE ONLINE AT **www.leonaur.com**
AND FROM ALL GOOD BOOK STORES

07/09

# ALSO FROM LEONAUR

**AVAILABLE IN SOFTCOVER OR HARDCOVER WITH DUST JACKET**

**ESCAPE FROM THE FRENCH** *by Edward Boys*—A Young Royal Navy Midshipman's Adventures During the Napoleonic War.

**THE VOYAGE OF H.M.S. PANDORA** *by Edward Edwards R. N. & George Hamilton, edited by Basil Thomson*—In Pursuit of the Mutineers of the Bounty in the South Seas—1790-1791.

**MEDUSA** *by J. B. Henry Savigny and Alexander Correard and Charlotte-Adélaïde Dard* —Narrative of a Voyage to Senegal in 1816 & The Sufferings of the Picard Family After the Shipwreck of the Medusa.

**THE SEA WAR OF 1812 VOLUME 1** *by A. T. Mahan*—A History of the Maritime Conflict.

**THE SEA WAR OF 1812 VOLUME 2** *by A. T. Mahan*—A History of the Maritime Conflict.

**WETHERELL OF H. M. S. HUSSAR** *by John Wetherell*—The Recollections of an Ordinary Seaman of the Royal Navy During the Napoleonic Wars.

**THE NAVAL BRIGADE IN NATAL** *by C. R. N. Burne*—With the Guns of H. M. S. Terrible & H. M. S. Tartar during the Boer War 1899-1900.

**THE VOYAGE OF H. M. S. BOUNTY** *by William Bligh*—The True Story of an 18th Century Voyage of Exploration and Mutiny.

**SHIPWRECK!** *by William Gilly*—The Royal Navy's Disasters at Sea 1793-1849.

**KING'S CUTTERS AND SMUGGLERS: 1700-1855** *by E. Keble Chatterton*—A unique period of maritime history-from the beginning of the eighteenth to the middle of the nineteenth century when British seamen risked all to smuggle valuable goods from wool to tea and spirits from and to the Continent.

**CONFEDERATE BLOCKADE RUNNER** *by John Wilkinson*—The Personal Recollections of an Officer of the Confederate Navy.

**NAVAL BATTLES OF THE NAPOLEONIC WARS** *by W. H. Fitchett*—Cape St. Vincent, the Nile, Cadiz, Copenhagen, Trafalgar & Others.

**PRISONERS OF THE RED DESERT** *by R. S. Gwatkin-Williams*—The Adventures of the Crew of the Tara During the First World War.

**U-BOAT WAR 1914-1918** *by James B. Connolly/Karl von Schenk*—Two Contrasting Accounts from Both Sides of the Conflict at Sea D uring the Great War.

**AVAILABLE ONLINE AT www.leonaur.com**
**AND FROM ALL GOOD BOOK STORES**

07/09

# ALSO FROM LEONAUR

**AVAILABLE IN SOFTCOVER OR HARDCOVER WITH DUST JACKET**

**IRON TIMES WITH THE GUARDS** *by An O. E. (G. P. A. Fildes)*—The Experiences of an Officer of the Coldstream Guards on the Western Front During the First World War.

**THE GREAT WAR IN THE MIDDLE EAST: 1** *by W. T. Massey*—The Desert Campaigns & How Jerusalem Was Won---two classic accounts in one volume.

**THE GREAT WAR IN THE MIDDLE EAST: 2** *by W. T. Massey*—Allenby's Final Triumph.

**SMITH-DORRIEN** *by Horace Smith-Dorrien*—Isandlwhana to the Great War.

**1914** *by Sir John French*—The Early Campaigns of the Great War by the British Commander.

**GRENADIER** *by E. R. M. Fryer*—The Recollections of an Officer of the Grenadier Guards throughout the Great War on the Western Front.

**BATTLE, CAPTURE & ESCAPE** *by George Pearson*—The Experiences of a Canadian Light Infantryman During the Great War.

**DIGGERS AT WAR** *by R. Hugh Knyvett & G. P. Cuttriss*—"Over There" With the Australians by R. Hugh Knyvett and Over the Top With the Third Australian Division by G. P. Cuttriss. Accounts of Australians During the Great War in the Middle East, at Gallipoli and on the Western Front.

**HEAVY FIGHTING BEFORE US** *by George Brenton Laurie*—The Letters of an Officer of the Royal Irish Rifles on the Western Front During the Great War.

**THE CAMELIERS** *by Oliver Hogue*—A Classic Account of the Australians of the Imperial Camel Corps During the First World War in the Middle East.

**RED DUST** *by Donald Black*—A Classic Account of Australian Light Horsemen in Palestine During the First World War.

**THE LEAN, BROWN MEN** *by Angus Buchanan*—Experiences in East Africa During the Great War with the 25th Royal Fusiliers—the Legion of Frontiersmen.

**THE NIGERIAN REGIMENT IN EAST AFRICA** *by W. D. Downes*—On Campaign During the Great War 1916-1918.

**THE 'DIE-HARDS' IN SIBERIA** *by John Ward*—With the Middlesex Regiment Against the Bolsheviks 1918-19.

AVAILABLE ONLINE AT **www.leonaur.com**
AND FROM ALL GOOD BOOK STORES

07/09

# ALSO FROM LEONAUR

## AVAILABLE IN SOFTCOVER OR HARDCOVER WITH DUST JACKET

**THE 9TH—THE KING'S (LIVERPOOL REGIMENT) IN THE GREAT WAR 1914 - 1918** *by Enos H. G. Roberts*—Mersey to mud—war and Liverpool men.

**THE GAMBARDIER** *by Mark Severn*—The experiences of a battery of Heavy artillery on the Western Front during the First World War.

**FROM MESSINES TO THIRD YPRES** *by Thomas Floyd*—A personal account of the First World War on the Western front by a 2/5th Lancashire Fusilier.

**THE IRISH GUARDS IN THE GREAT WAR - VOLUME 1** *by Rudyard Kipling*—Edited and Compiled from Their Diaries and Papers—The First Battalion.

**THE IRISH GUARDS IN THE GREAT WAR - VOLUME 1** *by Rudyard Kipling*—Edited and Compiled from Their Diaries and Papers—The Second Battalion.

**ARMOURED CARS IN EDEN** *by K. Roosevelt*—An American President's son serving in Rolls Royce armoured cars with the British in Mesopatamia & with the American Artillery in France during the First World War.

**CHASSEUR OF 1914** *by Marcel Dupont*—Experiences of the twilight of the French Light Cavalry by a young officer during the early battles of the great war in Europe.

**TROOP HORSE & TRENCH** *by R.A. Lloyd*—The experiences of a British Lifeguardsman of the household cavalry fighting on the western front during the First World War 1914-18.

**THE EAST AFRICAN MOUNTED RIFLES** *by C.J. Wilson*—Experiences of the campaign in the East African bush during the First World War.

**THE LONG PATROL** *by George Berrie*—A Novel of Light Horsemen from Gallipoli to the Palestine campaign of the First World War.

**THE FIGHTING CAMELIERS** *by Frank Reid*—The exploits of the Imperial Camel Corps in the desert and Palestine campaigns of the First World War.

**STEEL CHARIOTS IN THE DESERT** *by S. C. Rolls*—The first world war experiences of a Rolls Royce armoured car driver with the Duke of Westminster in Libya and in Arabia with T.E. Lawrence.

**WITH THE IMPERIAL CAMEL CORPS IN THE GREAT WAR** *by Geoffrey Inchbald*—The story of a serving officer with the British 2nd battalion against the Senussi and during the Palestine campaign.

www.ingramcontent.com/pod-product-compliance
Lightning Source LLC
Chambersburg PA
CBHW032052080426
42733CB00006B/242

* 9 7 8 1 8 4 6 7 7 9 0 3 9 *